AF437560

Praise for

FEARLESS FEEDBACK

"Most management books spend a lot of time telling you why feedback matters. Katie O'Brien Ceccarini's *Fearless Feedback* actually teaches you how. Every framework, every scenario, every piece of sample language is immediately usable—you finish a chapter and you can walk into your next conversation with genuine confidence. This is the book I wish every manager had access to from day one."

—JAMI ZAKEM, Executive Coach & Advisor

"While *Fearless Feedback* in many ways is a 'how to,' it starts with the origins of 'how come.' Katie rightly identifies that most leaders are not trained in feedback and with that lack of training comes fear of giving it. We have to start with the why, and she does an amazing job of speaking specifically to why feedback changes everything, even when it's hard. She gives practical models and scripts for how each leader can execute specific and timely feedback and shows the importance of how that impacts your team and also grows you as a leader. What makes this specifically unique to me is that I have seen her execute this in practice. These are not ideas of leadership from someone who hasn't been in the trenches for years; there are true examples and exercises that I have seen her implement and have challenged me to develop as a leader."

—NICK FIEDLER, VP, Customer Success

"This book is SO psychologically safe. This is the future of high-performing organizations—having standards, with a very human touch. Millennial approved."

—CHRISTIE HOFFMAN, Founder of Corporate Christie

"*Fearless Feedback* shows leaders how to master one of the most important skills for anyone committed to their team and to meaningful results. This book removes the anxiety and guesswork from hard conversations and offers practical tools you can use right away to build confidence. If you want better outcomes, deeper trust, and a more human way to lead and uplift others, this book is for you."

—BONNIE DAVIS, author of *Still Human: How to Build Organizations Where Leaders and Teams Thrive with AI*

"This book is especially refreshing because it skips the 'novel' and gets straight to the brass tacks of management. What stood out most was the reminder that feedback is a kindness, not a punishment. If you want to stop overthinking tough conversations and start supporting your team with clear, human feedback, read this."

—REBECCA VERHOEFF, Leader, Project & Program Management

"This is not just another leadership book. It's practical and to the point and will elevate your management in no time!"

—DAN HAMMOND, Cofounder & Chief Product Officer, Squadify

"*Fearless Feedback* is a standout book for giving managers the tools for doing right by both their organization and their team members. I would recommend it for managers looking to balance caring deeply for their team members while holding them accountable."

—EMILY LUCHSINGER, AI Agent Deployment Architect

"*Fearless Feedback* is a wonderful guide for any manager looking to lead with both heart and purpose. The relatable scenarios and personal stories offer an easy-to-follow 'how-to' that aligns perfectly with the emotional intelligence needed to support and inspire all generations, especially our youngest: Gen Z and Gen Alpha. I would recommend this to anyone seeking to build a culture of trust and genuine connection in the modern workforce."

—REGINA LYNCH, Membership, Sales & Operations Leader

"*Fearless Feedback* is an excellent book for managers that offers carefully constructed advice. The analysis of real-life situations makes

the next steps compelling, reasonable, and clearly effective. I especially appreciated the dive into the difficult situations where coaching was not embraced and how managers can navigate a path to a
positive solution or a decision to part ways."

—CHRISTINE STREP, Customer Success Manager

"What feels different about this book is that it is grounded in real-life
stories and experiences. The actual feedback conversations helped
me see what I had been doing wrong in the past."

—LEAH STALLONE, Founder of The Career Edit

FEARLESS FEEDBACK

Everything Managers Have Never Been Taught About Feedback

KATIE O'BRIEN CECCARINI

Endurance Management Coaching, LLC

Published by
  Endurance Management Coaching, LLC

Cover design and interior design by
  Claudine Mansour Design

Printed in the United States of America

979-8-9952360-1-6 hardcover
979-8-9952360-0-9 paperback

In memory of Lydia Mutch Carbonar
my first mentor and forever my frienc
I know you'd be over the moon proud of
You are deeply missed.

To my son, Wyatt,
who I hope always remembers that we a
people who dare to do hard things.

CONTENTS

PREFACE

In 2004, I was a first-time manager.

I had a part-time staff of tutors. A family came to me expressing concerns about one of our tutors, telling me the kids thought she was grouchy and mean.

I told my program director, Lydia, about the complaint.

She said, *"You need to give Sarah that feedback."*

Out of my mouth came, *"Okay, I'll talk to her when she comes in on Wednesday."* I didn't dare let Lydia think I wasn't ready or capable.

In my mind, I freaked out, *"How am I supposed to tell an older woman that kids think she's mean?"*

A few months later, I had a full-time employee who perpetually arrived late to work. She'd stroll in ten to fifteen minutes late with a pastry and latte in hand, seemingly oblivious and unbothered to how her lateness impacted everyone else's schedule. It drove me nuts.

On top of inconveniencing the rest of our team, she'd put on her timecard that she'd arrived at 10:30, but she really hadn't started work until 10:45. It felt dishonest and inconsiderate.

I raised it to my regional manager.

She said, *"Just give her feedback that she needs to be on time and be honest with her timekeeping."*

Again, my overwhelmed brain thought, *"Okay, but how do I say that without her thinking I'm a tyrant micromanager?"*

What actually came out of my mouth was, *"Okay, makes sense."*

This, my friends, is why this book exists: to help managers like you know *how* to craft, approach, and deliver feedback, all in a way that preserves your relationship dynamics.

Thank you for being here. Thank you for investing in yourself. And thank you for letting me be part of your career development journey.

INTRODUCTION

Fearless Feedback is going to change your relationship with feedback. You are going to finish this book better equipped to broach, address, and navigate feedback conversations. You are going to have a new sense of confidence, feel more calm, be less anxious, and find yourself a more capable manager.

By extension, you will begin to see stronger team performance, greater career development for your people, and elevated employee engagement.

Most managers aren't taught how to have great feedback conversations.

Until now.

Feedback is information that helps someone be their best. It's central to your core responsibility as a manager and leader to create the conditions for success for your people. You will not manage performance, provide career development, or deepen engagement without it.

Feedback is more than course correction.

Clear and actionable feedback is what helps your lower performers know how to grow further into their role. Purposeful and nuanced feedback elevates your top people to unlock their next level. Specific and timely feedback communicates the extent to which you value (and are invested in) every single person in your charge.

The bulk of what you're going to read focuses on the more

difficult end of the feedback spectrum. It's important to call out because this is intentional although not proportional.

Giving recognition and appreciation, two elements of positive feedback, are indispensable to your success as a manager. People need much more than we often assume and certainly more than most managers remember to give. In fact, Gallup research finds that only 23% of workers strongly agree they receive enough recognition for their efforts—meaning the vast majority of your people are likely hungry for it[1].

It's also true that you move the needle more with positive reinforcement than with corrective conversations. I've always believed this to be true, and it has been a core feature of my own management over the last two decades. The data backs up my experience: 67% of employees are engaged when their manager focuses on their strengths. Guess what happens when managers focus on weaknesses instead? That number collapses to just 2%[2].

As you begin your reading journey and see the primary focus is on addressing more critical feedback, know that it's because of the discomfort most managers have in this area, not because intentional, positive feedback is less important.

WHO THIS BOOK IS FOR

I wrote this book for the manager who wants to share feedback and is committed to doing it well. This is for the manager who puts off feedback conversations out of fear for how the

---

1 Benjamin Erikson-Farr, "The Power of Meaningful Recognition Using Clifton-Strengths," Gallup (2023) https://www.gallup.com/cliftonstrengths/en/545102/power-meaningful-recognition-using-cliftonstrengths.aspx

2 Brandon Rigoni and Jim Asplund, "Strengths-Based Employee Development: The Business Results," *Gallup* (2016) https://www.gallup.com/workplace/236297/strengths-based-employee-development-business-results.aspx

other person will react or the manager who feels awkward and unsure about how to bring up a feedback conversation.

From first-time manager to seasoned manager, my work and experience has shown the worries, assumptions, and self-doubt that persist in the area of difficult conversations does not discriminate based on title and level.

You're reading the right book if any of these thoughts have crossed your mind:

- Nothing's going to change, so why bother?

- If I give this feedback, it'll ruin our relationship.

- How the heck am I supposed to give that feedback?

I encourage you to take note of where you are in your relationship with feedback. On a scale of one to five, rate yourself:

- Overall comfort giving specific critical feedback

- Level of stress and anxiety approaching a feedback conversation

Then, when you finish this book, compare notes. What's changed? What's shifted? An investment in your development as a manager is a direct investment in the people on your team.

WHAT TO EXPECT

Fearless Feedback is designed to be highly practical, relatable, and tactical.

This is not a book on why feedback is important. You already know it is. This is a book focused on the *how*: how to have meaningful feedback conversations while preserving your relationships.

You are going to learn frameworks that are easily repeatable, meaning you can use this book to flip open whenever you need, get a refresher, and jump purposefully into an effective feedback conversation.

You are going to read about the nuances no one teaches: secondhand feedback, what to do when feedback hasn't been implemented, how to think about if it's time to let someone go, what to do when personal life impacts professional performance, and more.

The stories and scenarios you're going to read are a cross section of my own and those of managers I've coached and trained, and I believe they'll resonate deeply. With each language model, you will also gain the subtle insights that can help you feel more confident as you tackle situations and opportunities with your people.

HOW YOU'LL GET THERE

Part 1 is about understanding the Fearless Feedback Framework and the supporting frameworks that can enable your success.

You will see how the parts of the framework build upon one another.

We begin by clarifying the purpose of the conversation needing to be had. You will learn how to identify whether it's a conversation about an Instance, a Pattern, or Role Fit.

2 Pattern

A conversation focused on highlighting a **pattern of performance/behavior** that should change to enable greater success for your team member.

3 Role Fit

When Patterns persist or improvement is not keeping pace with business needs, the discussion is open and honest and focused on the extent to which they're a fit for the role.

1 Instance

Reacting to something you've seen, heard, or been made aware of.

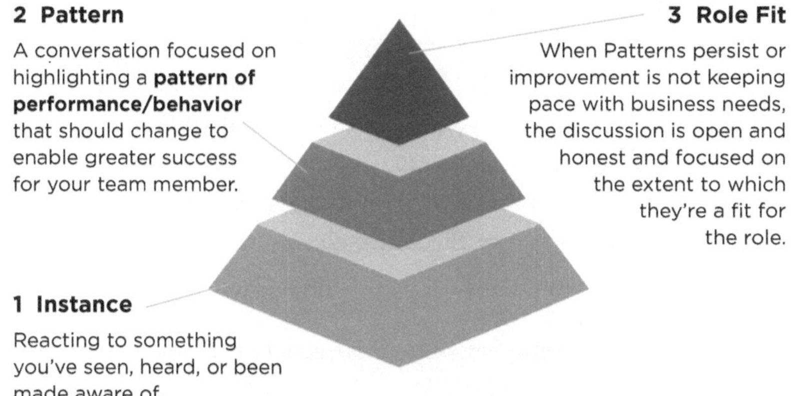

With feedback type identified, you'll move into the Fearless Feedback Framework and the three ingredients you need for a thoughtful and rewarding feedback conversation: Mindset, Relationship, and Delivery.

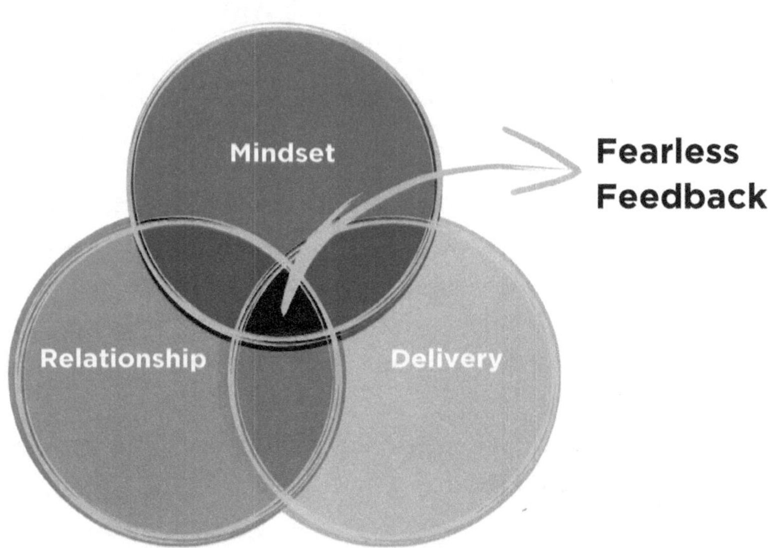

Throughout the book, you will see how we go back to each of these three ingredients in every situation.

Within Delivery, I will teach you the Headline, Observation, Ask (HOA) framework for feedback delivery.

This framework ensures you capture their interest and minimize reactions, to ultimately share an observation that will be actionable for their growth and development.

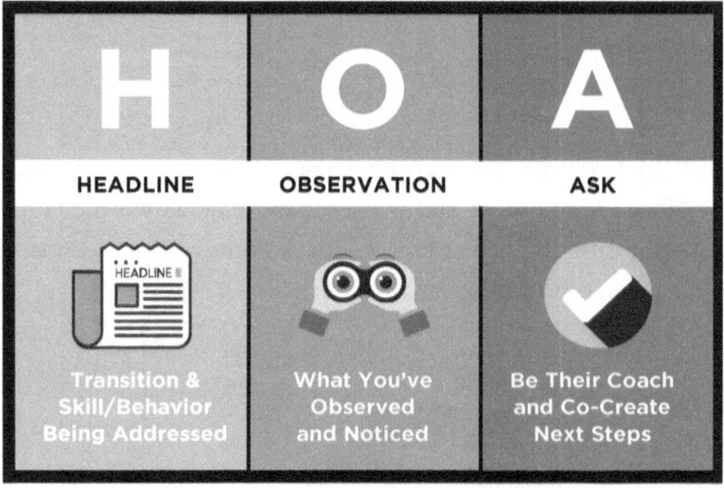

Next, you will gain tools and one last framework for handling reactions to feedback. Whether your message is met with silence, excuses, anger, or defensiveness, you will learn how to embrace the reaction, channel the energy, and then redirect it to the task at hand, which can impact future performance and behavior.

For a quick visual preview, this will be your framework for navigating reactions:

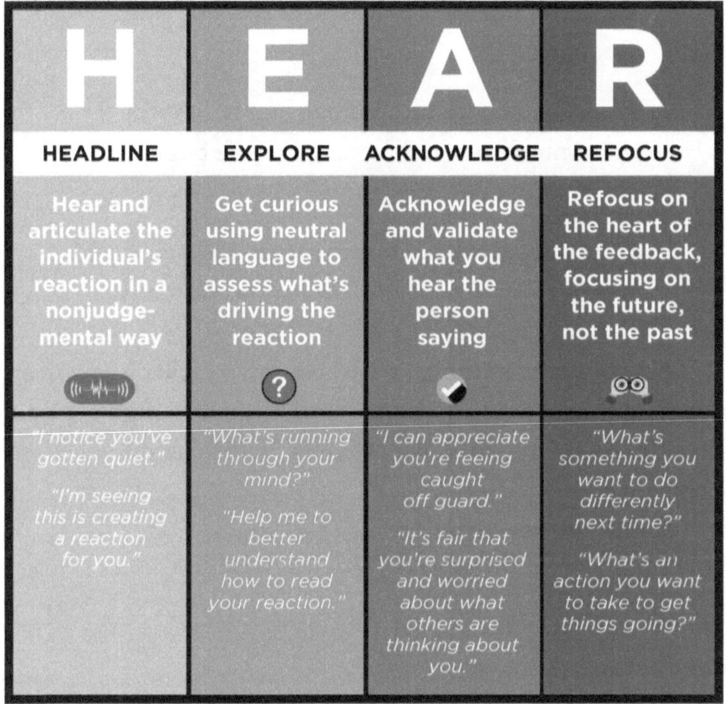

As the last component for Part 1, you have two chapters dedicated to bringing these frameworks to life by way of modeling language for real feedback situations. You'll see they're broken out first by the purpose of the feedback (Instance, Pattern, or Role Fit). Then we consciously think about our Mindset and Relationship, and finally we get tactical with using Headline, Observation, Ask (HOA) for your Delivery.

Part 2 is all about the additional nuances and challenges within these conversations.

- Knowing what to do and say after you've had the conversation

- Determining what to do about second hand feedback

- Learning how to be a human and hold folks accountable when their personal life begins to impact their performance

- Giving feedback to your manager and peers, and more!

This book is everything I wish I'd known earlier in my management journey. As you have questions and thoughts, please don't hesitate to email me directly (katie@enduranceboss.com).

Let our journey begin!

Introducing the Fearless Feedback Framework

PURPOSE OF FEEDBACK

Managers have a lot on their plates. Their ability to create a favorable environment for themselves, their people, their stakeholders, and the business is no small feat. It requires an intentional blend of both management and leadership skills.

For the sake of this book remaining focused on practical management tactics (vs. broader leadership), I'm going to zero in on the role feedback plays within these three core functions of a manager:

- Performance management

- Career development

- Employee retention

Feedback is what ensures you're managing performance and maintaining accountability for goals and deliverables. Feedback is what we lean into to highlight growth opportunities to help accelerate career growth. Feedback is also a tool that can help your people feel connected, motivated, and valued—all crucial keys to preventing attrition.

That is why, before we can talk about how to give feedback, we need to address the first challenge managers face: *"Should I share this feedback?"*

To answer that, you need to clarify the purpose and the type of feedback conversation to be had.

There are three types of feedback conversation: Instance, Pattern, and Role Fit. These represent a progression, a natural way to elevate urgency for implementation and improvement.

Once you've identified what type of feedback is on your hands, it becomes much more clear whether it's feedback that would be beneficial.

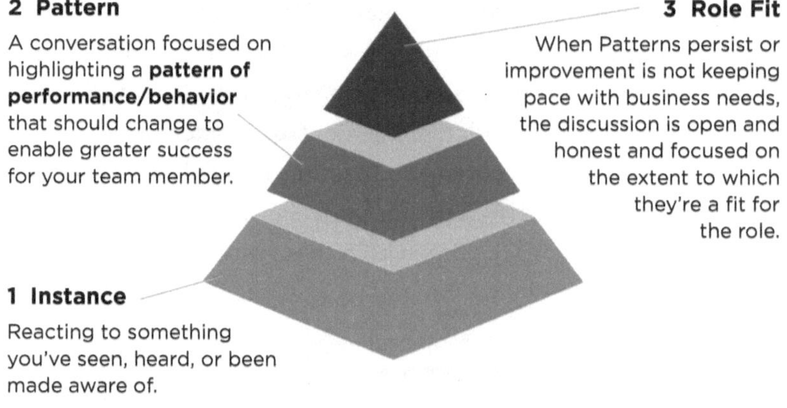

INSTANCE

At the heart of these conversations is an instance of performance, behavior, or engagement that would benefit from being done differently in the future.

The bulk of feedback conversations should be Instance conversations, hence being the base of the pyramid and the foundation that all feedback conversations should be built upon.

These conversations are sparked by something happening. A team member lost their cool in a meeting. They were late to an important presentation. They missed a deliverable. They were snarky to a team member. They were passive aggressive during a team announcement.

In the context of performance management, Instance conversations are how you "hold someone accountable." They miss the mark, so you provide timely coaching to help them course correct.

We can have positive Instance conversations as well. A team member killed it on a project. They were selfless when the team was in a pinch. They modeled curiosity during a large change announcement.

PATTERN

Pattern conversations are a natural escalation from Instance and are a powerful tool in a manager's toolbelt.

It's your ability to diagnose a situation as a Pattern that helps you break the Groundhog's Day cycle of feedback.

You know this cycle: the conversation you've had before, the feedback you've already shared, and the feeling of frustration that you need to have the same conversation again.

Sound familiar? Yes, of course!

Here's the key: don't have the same conversation again.

Pattern conversations are not about talking about something that happened again. Pattern conversations shift the discussion from *"This just happened again"* to *"There's a pattern that needs to change."*

The identification of a pattern also strengthens your

conviction to address the situation. Then, as you'll see, we literally use the word *pattern* in our delivery because it properly represents what we're discussing, and it sends a message of greater urgency for them to take action.

To give a quick preview, we'll use phrasing like this to address the feedback as a pattern:

- "There's a pattern related to your performance metrics I'm wanting us to dig into."

- "I'm noticing a pattern forming related to change announcements."

- "I'm picking up on a pattern with your engagement and want to connect to ensure you're set up to thrive."

Patterns can take two forms: obvious and not so obvious.

Obvious patterns are those in which the same performance or behavior is repeated. Missed metrics yet again. Spoke poorly of a customer again. Threw someone under the bus again. These are easier to see, so therefore, they are easier to diagnose as a pattern to address.

In the context of positive feedback, patterns might be steady willingness to mentor others, multiple months of consistent inputs, reliability with a problem-solving mentality.

The not-so-obvious patterns are about connecting dots between individual instances.

I remember having a new hire in our Chicago office. She didn't attend the new hire happy hour. That was an Instance, and I didn't bring it up because it wasn't a required event.

Then our VP was in town, and this new hire sat way in the back of the room. Again, not an issue, just odd as every other new hire was in the front row and eager to meet our VP. It was another instance but nothing fundamentally wrong or detrimental to her growth.

Then the following week she was showing some resistance to a training exercise. During that training, dots started to connect in my mind. Was she not invested in this new job? Was it different from what she was expecting?

Each event was not an issue in itself, so I didn't have the Instance conversations. When viewed holistically, there was a Pattern of potential disengagement.

When I approached her, I opened like this:

> *Could I steal a few minutes of your time? I'd like to get curious with you about a pattern with your engagement that I'm noticing and see what pivots we might need to make to help you as you're ramping up in this role.*

Good thing I did. I learned that she is the caretaker for her nephew. As soon as work is done, she needs to beeline it home, so her sister can head to work.

The not-so-obvious patterns might not yield concerns that need to be addressed, but they can bring greater clarity and get ahead of any assumptions you're at risk of making.

ROLE FIT

These conversations are much less frequent than Instance and Pattern.

This is when the heart of your conversation is openly and honestly discussing the extent to which they're a fit for their role.

Perhaps you've been working with them on taking more initiative and authority of their work, and you're not seeing progress. Perhaps they've been working really hard on their priority management, yet things are still slipping through the cracks.

You might even have a scenario where their attitude has continued to deteriorate to the point that it's affecting their performance and relationships within the business.

The key here is this: this conversation should never be a surprise.

You've been having Instance and Pattern conversations over the last number of weeks or months, and you're not seeing traction. In my experience, if you've been consistent with Instance and Pattern conversations, and they're still struggling, this conversation can come as a relief.

For scenarios of positive feedback, Role Fit conversations can explore how they might have outgrown their responsibilities and may be ready to take on more. Or perhaps it's a conversation encouraging them to apply to another role within the organization that would challenge them and accelerate their growth.

INFORMING YOUR DECISION

Once you've identified the purpose and type of feedback, you can begin determining whether it should be shared.

Below are helpful questions to ask when reflecting on an Instance situation:

- Would I want to know?

- How will this feedback serve their performance?

- In what ways is this feedback aligned with their aspirations?

- In what ways does this feedback impact the team and / or stakeholder experiences?

Asking yourself these questions tends to bring you to a pretty clear *yes* or *no*.

If you need additional conviction whether to raise this conversation, ask yourself this: *If this turns into a pattern, will that pattern serve them?*

When you've identified a scenario of a Pattern, these questions can help in your decision-making:

- Would I want to know?

- If I say nothing, what will happen? Will that serve them and the team?

- In what ways will this pattern get in the way of their future success?

- How is this pattern impacting their standing with their stakeholders?

COMMON MANAGER QUESTION

At this stage, it's natural that managers have this question: *"Is it okay to have a Pattern conversation if I haven't had an Instance conversation?"*

Until now, the concepts of Instance, Pattern, and Role Fit conversation likely haven't crossed your mind.

Here's the short answer: yes, it's okay to have a Pattern conversation if you haven't had an Instance conversation. That being said, your life will be easier if from here on out you minimize the times you skip the Instance interaction.

Think of it this way: Is it easier to let someone know they have food in their teeth when it's just one piece of lettuce wedged between teeth? Or is it better to wait until there's more food there to let them know?

CHAPTER SUMMARY

Before the internal debate begins about whether you should share feedback, zoom out and determine the purpose of the conversation.

There are three types of feedback conversations:

- **Instance**: You are addressing something that happened with the intention to impact future behavior.

- **Pattern**: You're elevating the urgency of the conversation by highlighting a pattern of performance and behavior.

- **Role Fit**: When you begin to have concerns about their ability to be successful in the role, an honest and open dialogue might be needed, particularly if progress and traction from previous feedback conversations has been minimal.

MINDSET

Fearless Feedback is about saying what ought to be said without fear of damaging your relationship.

There are three elements that go into this model: Mindset, Relationship, and Delivery.

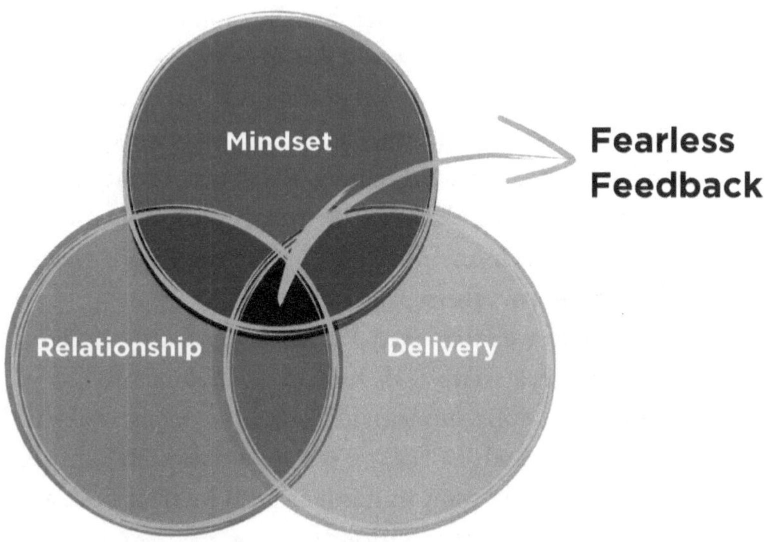

When you operate at the intersection of these three, you become the manager who is known for delivering great team performance, developing strong team members, and creating an engaging culture of safety and growth.

The first place to start is Mindset.

My starting place for getting my head in the game for a feedback conversation is my leadership style, which is, "Be human, with standards."

In 2019, I was interviewing to fill the manager trainer role on my team. I was looking for someone who could take over running monthly manager training and to develop a leadership development program for high-potential individual contributors.

I interviewed Andrea and ultimately hired her, and she did a fantastic job.

Fast forward to January 2021 when I was leaving my role as head of learning and development. In our one-to-one meeting, Andrea said to me, *"You probably don't remember this, but when you interviewed me, I asked you what your leadership style was."*

I responded, *"Yeah, and what did I say?"* giving her a smile because I genuinely didn't remember the moment.

Andrea said, *"You told me your style was human—that you meet people where they are and believe that work is a part of life but not our whole life. It was that moment I knew I wanted to work for you."*

To tell you my heart was bursting with warm fuzzies would be an understatement. I hadn't remembered that moment, and to know how much one moment, one response can change someone and impact them, was a blessing.

As the years have progressed, I've now consciously modified my leadership style to this: "Be human, with standards."

Here's why: I don't fundamentally believe people wake up and think to themselves, *"Let me just be mediocre."* It's my experience that people want to do their best, be their best, and make themselves and others proud.

Through that lens, I feel it's my responsibility to hold people to the standards I know they are capable of. Doing anything less is a disservice to them and disrespectful to their talents.

In the day to day, I bring this leadership style to life by funneling everything through the following three guiding principles. These shape my Mindset, enabling me to step fully into the Fearless Feedback Framework:

1. Care deeply.

2. Hold a high bar.

3. Focus on strengths and energizing work.

CARE DEEPLY

Caring deeply for the people in your charge means caring for their wellbeing and prioritizing their needs. It also means caring enough to have the conversation. Caring enough to highlight where they're missing the mark. Caring enough to ensure they feel valued. Caring enough to say what needs to be said so they can be their best and do their best.

It is easier said than done, which is why it is the first filter through which I ask myself, *"If I cared deeply for their well-being and development, would I share this feedback?"*

And yes, the caring thing to do is to share your observation, directly and with care.

HOLD A HIGH BAR

A moment ago I shared that I don't believe people wake up thinking, *"I'll just be mediocre today."*

When you hold a low bar, guess what? That's where people stay. Then you're constantly managing from a place of disappointment.

When you hold an appropriately high bar, guess what? People rise to the occasion.

There's a spiel every single person who has reported to me in the last fifteen years has heard. It goes like this:

> *I hold an incredibly high bar but never higher than what I believe you can reach and what I can coach you to.*

It's a commitment I make to every person I have the privilege of leading. I'm going to hold a high bar, not an unrealistic bar of excellence, a bar I know they're capable of, particularly with my coaching and support.

When I'm considering whether an Instance, a Pattern, or Role Fit warrants a feedback conversation, I strengthen my Mindset by asking, *"If I don't share this, am I lowering their bar?"*

Very often the right thing to do is to hold each person to a standard of excellence, not just for me or the business but for them, their pride, their growth, and their career progression.

The principle holds true for your best performers as well. They are the ones particularly hungry to raise their own bar, and you're in a position to help them do so.

These are powerful questions to help you reflect and identify meaningful feedback that you can then share that will help your top folks continue to raise their own high bar:

- What's their next level look and feel like?

- What would make them *even* better in their role?

- What's a skill or behavior that will serve them well in their next role?

- What's one skill or behavior I'd love to see them be 10% more confident with?

When you're in a headspace of believing in your people and seeing an opportunity to empower them to rise to the occasion, you're better positioned for Fearless Feedback.

FOCUS ON STRENGTHS AND ENERGIZING WORK

I've modified this principle and mindset in recent years.

I used to just say to Focus on Strengths. After all, according to Gallup, you're 6x more engaged in your work when you're using your strengths[3].

What experience has also shown me is that energizing work matters greatly. When you're energized to tackle something, you're more productive, efficient, curious, and open minded.

Understanding what energizes (and drains) my people became a core feature of my management approach. Every four to six weeks or so, it was a topic in one-to-one meetings. I'd ask different versions of this:

- What's energizing you these days?

- And what within that is energizing?

- And then what within that particularly lights you up?

Each follow-up question is like peeling back a layer of an onion, until you get to the true energizing activity.

When I know what energizes (and drains) my folks, I can make better decisions about delegation, goals, and more, all of which strengthens my ability to manage performance, provide

---

3 "Employees Who Use Their Strengths Outperform Those Who Don't," Gallup, 2015 https://www.gallup.com/workplace/236561/employees-strengths-outperform-don. aspx

career development, and ensure my folks are engaged in their work.

How this fits into Mindset and Fearless Feedback is two-fold:

1. Find ways to connect the feedback to a strength or energizing work.

2. Remember to look for the good.

A powerful question to ask yourself is, *"If I hold back on sharing this feedback, how am I impacting what energizes them?"*

Just about every person I've managed has been energized to become a better, stronger, more impactful version of themselves. Remembering that puts you in a powerful Mindset to approach the sharing of feedback.

ADDITIONAL ACTIONABLE TACTICS

If you're facing a more challenging situation and need additional tools to get you into a Mindset that will serve your effectiveness in a feedback conversation, here are three additional strategies to try.

TACTIC 1: DON'T CALL IT FEEDBACK

If saying, *"I need to have a feedback conversation with Libby,"* is freaking you out, stop using the word *feedback*.

Try this on for size instead: *"I have information that will help Libby succeed."*

That's literally what I do. I pause and consider what feedback is. **It's the sharing of an observation that is intended to help set up someone for more success.**

When you put it like that, what shifts in your brain?

In my brain and body, I feel a release. I think, *"Well in that case, it would be rude not to bring this up!"*

TACTIC 2: IMAGINE FOOD IN YOUR TEETH

In *Radical Candor*, Kim Scott uses the memorable metaphor of telling someone they have spinach in their teeth to illustrate the importance of giving feedback that is both kind and clear.

I want to take that relatable metaphor further in two important ways that contribute to strengthening our Mindset as we approach feedback.

1. Our desire to know

2. Our frustration when we don't

First, when you have food in your teeth, do you want someone to tell you?

Yes, absolutely. You first might have a tinge of embarrassment when someone kindly tells you before gratitude takes over because you can do something about it.

On the flip side, how do you feel when you discover you have food in your teeth, but no one told you?

Most of us have these reactions: *"Why didn't someone tell me?" "How long has it been there?" "I don't trust them as much now!"*

I share this because feedback is like having food in your teeth: others see it, and you don't.

The longer we don't say anything, the more "food" that racks up in their teeth.

TACTIC 3: REANCHOR YOUR ASSUMPTIONS

I piloted this strategy with a manager on my team back in 2012. Since then, it's been a staple in helping managers around the world to consciously adopt a mindset that can better serve their conversations.

Nora and I were in a conference room in the Yelp Scottsdale

office. Sitting comfortably on the navy couches, we were talking about how to give feedback to a new hire we weren't confident was equipped to do the account manager job.

Nora had some reasonable reservations because this new hire had demonstrated some defensive behaviors, and she knew she had to play this one carefully.

I asked, *"What's the worst-case scenario for his reaction?"*

She responded with something like, *"He gets super defensive, yells back at me, and blames me for the challenges I'm observing."*

I said, *"Okay, fair. Now, what's the best-case scenario?"*

I think this question surprised us both.

She said with a bit of a smirk, *"Hmm, I guess the best would be that he sees what I'm saying, immediately changes what he's doing, and is super grateful for me."*

Then I took it one step further by asking, *"Now, what's the middle-case scenario?"*

Nora, now seeing where I was going with this, shared, *"Middle case is maybe he doesn't like it, and he sees that I'm trying to help."*

BINGO.

Our minds automatically anchor to the worst-case scenario. Your job is to reanchor to the most probable scenario: the middle case.

The worst case rarely happens. The best case rarely happens. The most probable is the middle scenario, which is a combination of a reaction paired with an understanding of what we're trying to do, which is to help them succeed.

When you put your worst-case fears to the side, your more rational self is able to step forward, positioning you to have a more impactful conversation.

CHAPTER SUMMARY

You can more confidently approach and share feedback when your Mindset is in the right place.

Three guiding principles that can give you a strong foundation:

1. Care deeply.

2. Hold a high bar.

3. Focus on strengths and energizing work.

If your Mindset is still playing games with you, these three tactics can ensure your inner game is in service of your outer game:

- **Don't call it feedback**. You have information to share that will help this person be their best.

- **Imagine food in their teeth.** They want to know, and they'll be annoyed the longer they don't know.

- **Reanchor your assumptions.** The best and worst case rarely happen, so anchor to the middle, and most likely, scenario.

RELATIONSHIP

When I ask managers why they avoid having feedback conversations, the top response is this: *"I'm afraid of hurting our relationship."*

There's an assumption that sharing information, such as an observation of someone's performance or engagement, will negatively impact the relationship with that person.

In reality, caring, tough conversations can *strengthen* relationship dynamics in the long run. You become the manager they will always remember as helping them be the best version of themselves.

That's why, within the scope of the Fearless Feedback Framework, the Relationship element has two components:

- Create a strong foundation of a relationship.

- Maintain trust and safety within a conversation.

Here's how we're going to tackle both.

To create a strong foundation, use the tools in this chapter to impact your feedback conversations and change the way you manage (for the better).

To preserve trust and safety, expect a clear explanation starting in Chapter 6 when I highlight real-life feedback situations.

CREATE STRONG RELATIONSHIPS

If I could wave a magic wand and instantly have every manager be great at one conversation, it's this one.

Here's why: it's the foundation for everything—clarity, performance, engagement, retention, vulnerability, and trust. In our increasingly remote, virtual, and AI-driven world, the managers and companies that prioritize human connection will retain the best talent and deliver the best results.

This conversation enables you to minimize the guesswork, reduce assumptions, and establish alignment from the get-go.

There are three types of this conversation:

- Relationship Kickoff Conversation

- Former Peer Relationship Reset Conversation

- Relationship Reinvestment Conversation

Within this conversation, regardless of your audience, you will Set the Stage and then cover four topics:

- Personal

- Professional

- Alignment

- Aspirations

Most managers I work with feel confident with the first topic: getting to know more about team members and cross-functional partners on a personal level. Now you have an opportunity to build upon these and intentionally go deeper.

What follows is a sampling of questions for these conversations. Read through and be sure to highlight the ones that strike you most.

RELATIONSHIP KICKOFF CONVERSATION

You've got a brand new person joining your team, and they're new to the company. After meeting them in the interview process and ahead of your first real one-to-one meeting, you have this conversation. Remember, this is a back-and-forth conversation. They'll likely ask you questions in return. Your objective is mutual sharing for a strong relationship foundation.

Set the Stage

To help them know what to expect with this meeting, you can send them a simple note that might read like this:

Welcome to the team!

I'm invested in your growth and development, and I believe the best way to set us up for mutual success is to get to know one another.

I've just sent over an invite for us to connect. There's nothing for you to prepare, just bring yourself and maybe your favorite warm beverage.

I'm interested in getting to know you further, better understanding your career journey, talking through our communication preferences, and learning more about your aspirations—all of which will help us hit the ground running together.

Helping them to know what to expect sets the tone that this will be an open conversation and an opportunity to have a strong start in this new management relationship.

Personal Questions

- Where'd you grow up?

- Who are the important humans in your life? What are their names?

- Do you have any pets?

- What are your hobbies? Any favorite music or movies?

- What's something you wish a crystal ball could tell you?

Professional Questions

- What's been your journey that's landed you here?

- What did you love about your last role?

- What elements of your last role would you love to never do again?

- What type of work energizes you? What *within that* is especially energizing?

- What work tends to zap your energy? What *within that* feels especially draining?

What comes next is the meat and potatoes of the conversation, the part of the discussion where you feel clarity, alignment, and trust immediately start to grow. I don't ask *all* of these questions, nor should you. These are a sampling to illustrate the types of questions you can ask to create a solid foundation with a new team member.

Alignment Questions

- How do you like to be recognized?

- What gets you up in the morning after a tough day?

- When you're stressed, how might it impact how you communicate and engage?

- What's something for me to look for when your confidence is slipping, so I can support your development?

- What's been the most impactful feedback you've received?

- When you received feedback you didn't agree with, what about the delivery didn't work?

- What's been your experience with upward feedback?

- When we have urgent issues, what's important for us to align on ahead of time?

Notice the question I don't ask. I never ask, *"How do you like to receive feedback?"*

Here's why: the answer is typically useless. If that feels harsh, stick with me.

They may not know because they're newer to the workforce and aren't yet sure. Or, they tell you this: *"Just give it to me directly."*

When you give direct feedback, they get defensive. The conversation blows up, and you're scratching your head thinking, *"WTF, you said to give it to you directly!"*

Sound familiar? Yes, of course.

A more powerful approach is to ask them to think back to an example and then to make that a point of curiosity and discussion.

Your phrasing might sound like this:

As your new manager, my goal is to develop you and help you do the best work of your career. Sharing feedback is part of that journey. I want to be sure I share feedback in a way that lands and is actionable. I'm wanting to get curious about your experience with feedback.

Tell me about a time you received feedback that maybe was tough and you received it well. How was it delivered? What worked in that delivery?

[Pause to listen, and ask genuinely curious follow-up questions as needed. Remember, your goal is to understand their experiences and preferences, so you can meet them where they are and manage them effectively.]

Great, that's helpful. Now let's go to the other end of things. Tell me about a time you received feedback that's still a thorn in your side, something you didn't receive as well. How was it delivered? What didn't work with that delivery?

Speaking in terms of examples and experiences moves the conversation away from people saying what they *think* you want to hear and gives you insights that truly can enable you to share feedback more effectively.

Also, did you notice that one question in the list about

upward feedback? *What's been your experience with upward feedback?*

I started asking this question when I was head of learning and development at Opendoor. I'd noticed that my team was a bit less active in offering feedback to me than previous teams I'd worked with.

It struck me that there was a dual challenge happening:

- I wasn't asking for feedback in a specific enough manner.

- Some folks had previous experiences that taught them not to speak up.

We'll get to how to ask for feedback in Chapter 16. Here's a preview of the punchline: specific asks get specific answers. When you ask with specificity, you get more specific feedback. When you ask too broadly, you get nothing.

Two of my team members ultimately trusted me enough to tell me that a previous manager of theirs had asked for feedback, and each time they felt they ultimately were punished for sharing honest feedback. Their lived experience taught them, *"When a manager asks for feedback, just say everything is good."*

I began asking about their upward feedback experience in this conversation, so I could understand their lived experience and meet them where they are.

If you'd like to watch and listen to me leading the alignment portion of this conversation, visit www.fearlessfeedbackbook. com/resources. You'll notice the segment from 9:40–12:10 I'm asking about upward feedback experiences.

Finally, let's explore the last topic of discussion for the Relationship Kickoff Conversation.

Aspirations

This last part of the conversation is where you wind down and begin to understand their bigger picture. When you know the type of life they want to lead or what they'd do if they knew they wouldn't fail, you're better positioned to help them along their journey.

Plus, insight into their larger desires enables you to make your feedback more relevant.

Here are sample questions to guide this part of the discussion:

- What type of work do you hope will be on your plate next year? Three years from now?

- If money were no object, what would you do?

- If you knew you wouldn't fail, what would you do?

- What's important for me to help you grow in your career?

I had a training manager on my team who wanted to go back to school and be an interior designer. Knowing this made it easier for me to make feedback transferable. Priority management, stakeholder management, influence, and executive communication are all areas of development as a training manager *and* highly applicable to working with vendors, contractors, and clients as an interior designer.

FORMER PEER RELATIONSHIP
RESET CONVERSATION

When you're promoted, you're often in a position to begin managing your former peers. This transition is imperative, and the Former Peer Relationship Reset Conversation is a vital tool to set you up for mutually beneficial outcomes.

Set the Stage

As a first step, you ought to name the elephant in the room. There's no need to pretend that things are the same, and frankly everyone is curious about how things are going to be.

I recommend reaching out directly to each former peer with the following type of message. If you're in close proximity (same office or city), prioritize having this conversation in person. If they are a remote team member, seek to set up a virtual coffee. The key is that this is a casual, low-stress meeting.

> *Hey there! I was hoping you and I could grab a coffee this week.*
>
> *It's on my mind, and I'm assuming it's on yours as well, to recognize that our dynamic has shifted.*
>
> *I'd propose we chat through what this means for both of us and how we can both be set up for success in this next chapter.*

A few deliberate word choices to highlight:

- **Dynamic shifted**: This phrasing lands better than saying, *"Now that you report to me . . . "*

- **Success**: Make the success mutually beneficial. It's as much about you as it is about them.

- **Next chapter**: Thinking about work in terms of chapters helps because the nature of a chapter is there's a beginning, middle, and end, which can help reduce nervousness about the future.

Now that you've opened the door and set the scene, your job is to come into the conversation with a new lens.

How you engage, empower, and develop this person will impact their life satisfaction.

Yes, I said life satisfaction. A 2018 study of 38,000 people had this finding:

> Across the board, people who said they felt like their relationship with their work supervisor was more like that of partners, as opposed to one in which they felt like their supervisor was more of a traditional boss, were likely to report much greater life satisfaction.[4]

This is particularly important to remember when we're making the transition from peers to a management relationship. It's incredibly easy to avoid talking about the obvious or lean too heavily into being friends.

Here are the questions, in each of our four topics, that you can leverage during this transition.

Personal Questions

- What's the latest going on in your world?

- Remind me the names of your kids/partner.

- We've been working together for a while. What's something outside of work that's lighting you up these days?

---

4 Bill Murphy Jr., "A Massive New Study of 38,000 Workers Says This 1 Thing Makes Employees Much Happier (and Probably More Loyal)," Inc. (2018)

Professional Questions

- What work on your plate do you find most energizing? What *within that* is particularly invigorating?

- What work on your plate do you find most draining? What *within that* tends to put out your fire?

- What's something you're hungry to get exposure to?

- Who are folks around the business you're hoping to have greater visibility with?

Alignment Questions

- My goal is to help you be even more of your best. What elements of your work are you wanting more feedback on?

- Because it will be the first time I'm offering you feedback, what's best for me to keep in mind when approaching you with ideas and suggestions with your work?

- I've often seen your communication strengths to be xyz. What elements of your communication do you want to continue strengthening?

- What's one recommendation you might offer me to keep in mind when I'm communicating with the team?

- If/When our communication falters, what would feel good to align on now to make it easier for us to get back on track?

Aspiration Questions

- If you knew you wouldn't fail, what decision would you make?

- What type of work do you hope is on your plate a year from now?

- What impact do you hope your work has three years from now?

Leading this open and intentional conversation will give you an opportunity to establish your relationship on a new level, settling the nerves and concerns of each of you.

In the case that you're not only now managing a former peer, they are also a good friend, here is my top recommendation: align on what hat you're wearing.

Here's what I mean. You're in a one-to-one meeting, and you're chatting as friends. When you shift to talking about work, it can be as simple as saying, *"Okay, putting my work hat back on . . . "*

You may be hanging out at happy hour, and you're wanting to stay in friend mode, not manager mode. You can say, *"Tonight I've got my friend hat on . . . "*

With my very first promotion into a management role, I managed a friend from college, and she happened to be my roommate. We made an agreement. We could talk work on our commute back to our apartment (yes, we also commuted together some days), but only up until we hit the Golden Gate Bridge. As soon as we got to the San Francisco side of the bridge, work talk was done, and friend mode was activated.

RELATIONSHIP REINVESTMENT CONVERSATION

For folks you've never had a Relationship Kickoff Conversation with, or folks with whom it's been a long time since you did, this reinvestment conversation can be a powerful tool. The intention here is that you regularly reconnect, revisit, and realign to ensure you remain in lock step with how you're working together.

Set the Stage

Setting the stage for this conversation might sound like this:

> *Hello! One thing I'm committed to doing more of this year is reinvesting in my relationships around the org.*
>
> *We've been working together for a while, and we work well together. I don't want to take that for granted.*
>
> *If you're up for it, I'd vote for us to catch up personally and then talk about what else we can do to ensure we're set up for continued success with our communication and alignment.*
>
> *Sound good to you?*

The Relationship Reinvestment Conversation also hits on the same four topics, with slightly modified questions. And of course, neither this conversation nor the Relationship Kickoff Conversation should be treated as a checklist. Be human, be present, stay curious, and know directionally what you're hoping to uncover and align on.

Personal Questions

- [Lean into what you know of their hobbies and important people in their life.]

- What have been some personal highlights over the last six months?

- What's something you're reading/watching/listening to that you're loving?

Professional Questions

- What's lighting you up these days within your work?

- What are you noticing is more draining than it used to be?

- What do you see happening in your field in the next year?

Alignment Questions

- Which elements of our communication do we want to keep business as usual?

- If there were one thing I could do differently in the way I communicate with you, what might you suggest?

- When things are busy/urgent issues arise, I don't want to assume what I've been doing is best. What would be helpful to revisit about how we communicate in those times?

- When I have ideas or notice something that might make your life easier or work more impactful, what can I do differently from what I've been doing?

- In coming months, given the shifting dynamics within the org/industry, inevitably we will have

a difference of opinion. When that happens,
what feels important for how we respond in that
moment?

Aspiration Questions

- What type of work do you hope will be on your
  plate next year? Three years from now?

- If money were no object, what would you
  be doing?

COMMON MANAGER QUESTIONS

WHAT IF THEY DON'T KNOW HOW TO ANSWER THE ALIGNMENT QUESTIONS?

Most of us are not used to being asked these questions. That's what makes them so powerful. The questions require us to think and truly reflect. Holding space for them to pause, consider, and share is part of the trust and relationship building process.

You can also adjust your Set the Stage messaging to include more specifics on the topics and types of questions you may be asking when you two connect. The goal isn't to stump them, the goal is an open exploration in service of creating a strong foundation for your relationship.

WHAT DO I DO WITH THIS INFORMATION?

Each response in this conversation is a piece of gold added to a treasure chest of how to manage and work with this person.

There are two simple ways to capture and remember the insights you gain.

First, take notes after the conversation. In a doc that's private to you, log each team member's preferences—each nugget of gold—to easily reference when you need them.

Second, add key elements of your alignment discussion to the top of your running one-to-one agenda. They can live there and be seen each time you meet.

Until it becomes second nature to leverage the insights you've gained, reference these two sources to help you effectively communicate with them.

CHAPTER SUMMARY

The investment you make upfront in your relationships will pay dividends when the tough stuff comes up. Mastering these foundational relationship-building conversations and prioritizing trust and safety when you communicate is how you'll be able to meaningfully step into the Relationship component of the Fearless Feedback Framework.

These conversations start with Setting the Stage and then you intentionally connect via four topics:

- **Personal**: Who are they, and what's important to them?

- **Professional**: Where have they been, and what energizes them in their work?

- **Alignment**: How do you two want to communicate with one another?

- **Aspirations**: What are they wanting in their future?

DELIVERY

The last component to our Fearless Feedback Framework is Delivery.

Your Delivery encompasses your word choices, structure, clarity, and the overall packaging of your message. This is the area that understandably gets the most attention because your words, and how you deliver them, have impact and consequence.

What's also true is you have some wiggle room in your Delivery when your Mindset and Relationship are strong.

That's precisely why it would be a disservice to you, and your time, to jump straight to how to structure your feedback message without addressing the vital factors of getting your head in the game and the power of relationship in performance and development conversations.

This chapter introduces a simple, repeatable framework designed to make your Delivery of feedback conversations easier to start, clearer to message, and more likely to drive change.

HEADLINE, OBSERVATION, ASK

There are three components to the Headline, Observation, Ask (HOA) framework:

- The **Headline** transitions you into your conversation while also naming what it is you want to discuss.

- The **Observation** is where you objectively convey the behavior, performance challenge, or growth opportunity.

- The **Ask** is where you shift into being their coach by asking questions, listening, and helping build their awareness before guiding them to identify actions to be taken.

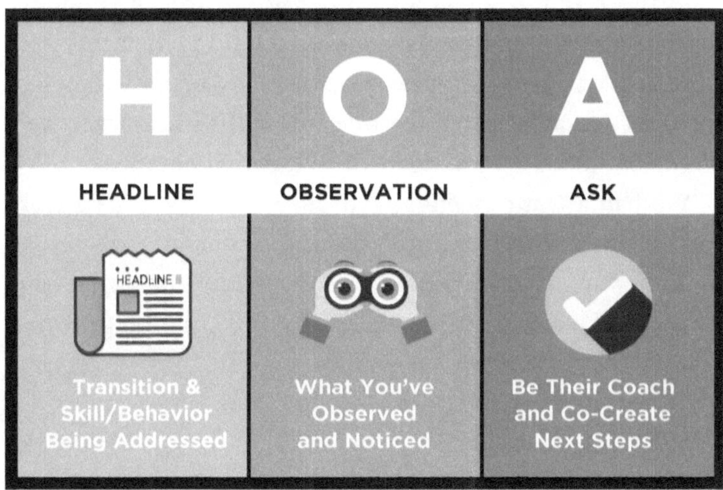

HOA is particularly effective and different than other frameworks for three key reasons:

1. The hardest part about a feedback conversation is the opening. This framework prioritizes it, giving you the tools to succeed.

2. Over-talking and beating around the bush deteriorates your message. This framework gives you confidence to speak clearly and with care about the observed behavior or performance.

3. Feedback without action is simply criticism. This framework ensures the feedback you share is actionable, never leaving someone wondering, *"What am I supposed to do with this?"*

Below is a quick demonstration of how HOA can sound.

In this scenario, I had a high performer who was hungry for promotion. Their hard skills were solid, and their soft skills were in need of maturity and steadiness. In a previous development conversation about their desire for their next level, we'd discussed stepping up as more of a leader within the team.

We had a team meeting, and I saw something new from them, something that if not addressed, would certainly get in their way of advancement and might turn into a Pattern. Through the lens of caring deeply for this person's growth, I approached the Delivery as follows.

Headline

I know how invested and hungry you are for your next level. I noticed something earlier that I want to highlight, so you can continue elevating your game. The area I want to dive into is leadership presence. Do you have a few minutes to connect?

Observation

During our team meeting today, I saw you had a reaction to the upcoming changes in how we're handling client fulfillment. Your body language sent a powerful message, and I don't believe it was the message you intended to send. Because the team looks up to you, and I know how committed you are to your development, I wanted to shine a light on this today as an opportunity for growth.

Ask

Let's start with getting curious and then chat through how you can strike a balance between staying true to how you're feeling while showing up as a leader who can impact those around you.

[Shift to Coach Mode.]

Can you connect back to that moment? What activated that response?

[Listen and encourage self-reflection.]

When you think about your brand as a leader within this team, what do you want that to be?

[Listen and stay curious.]

What actions contribute to creating that brand? Can you also see how today's actions inadvertently can detract from that brand?

[Listen and continue encouraging exploration.]

Let's assume there will be other times when you disagree or have an opportunity to react. What do you want to do differently next time that better aligns how you want to continue developing into your future roles?
In what ways would you like me to support you in this area?

Now let me break down each component of HOA (Headline, Observation, Ask) and the intentional methods you can leverage within each to maximize the impact of your message and drive real change and impact.

HEADLINE

How you open a feedback conversation sets the tone for the reaction you will get.

Kicking off a feedback conversation also happens to be the hardest part for most managers. I know it always was for me.

Let me first illustrate what a Headline is not:

Hey, can I give you some feedback?

If that sentence just spiked your heart rate, you're not alone.

Not long ago, I worked with a group of ~100 managers and leaders. We had a solid cross section of seasoned and newer managers.

During the session, I ran the following Zoom poll.

Which would you prefer to hear:

- Can I give you some feedback?

- I'm seeing a way for you to have a greater impact. Do you have a few minutes?

Check out the results:

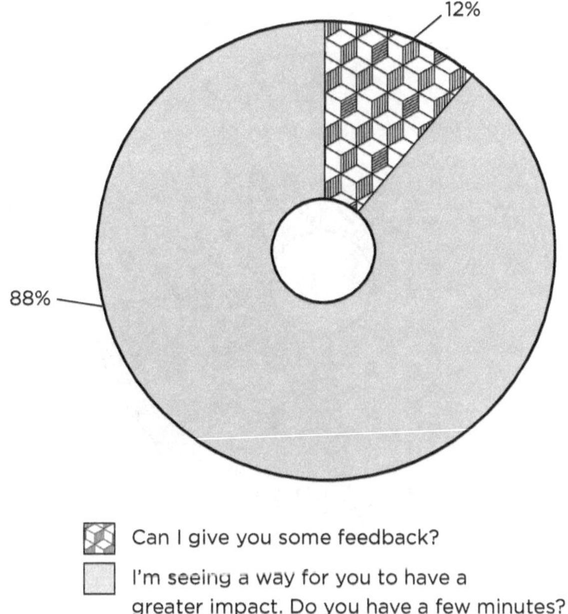

I've continued to use this poll with every audience I work with, and the results have remained consistent. Only 10–12% of my audiences prefer to hear, *"Can I give you some feedback?"*

Why is that?

This next data sampling is telling.

With the same group of ~100, I asked them to indicate the reaction they have when they hear, *"Can I give you some feedback?"* They were able to select multiple responses.

73% of the group had a reaction of *"What did I do?"* when they heard, *"Can I give you some feedback?"*

54% of the group also felt, *"Oh no."*

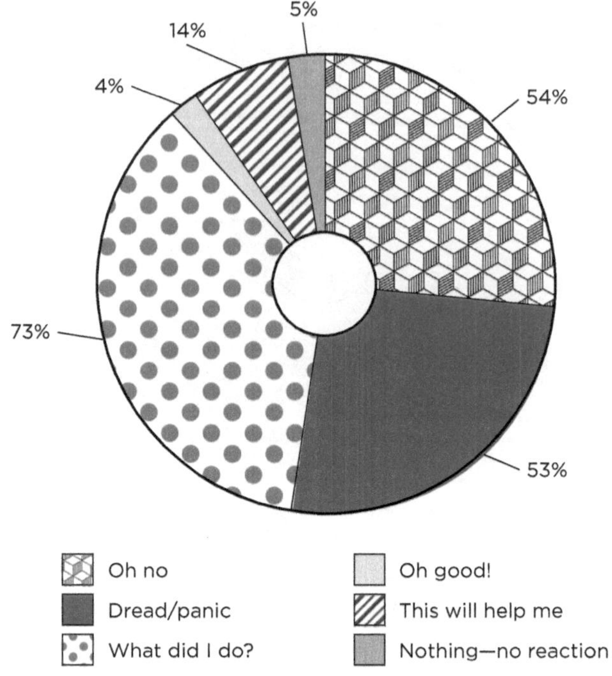

If we want to have better feedback conversations, we have to meet people where they are. People don't want the conversation to start with, *"Can I give you some feedback."*

There are three steps to prepare a strong Headline:

1. **Clarify Feedback Purpose**: Know the stage of the situation.

2. **Identify Name It to Tame It**: You can not tame what you can not name.

3. **Craft Transition**: The words you select to open the conversation matter.

HEADLINE STEP 1:
CLARIFY FEEDBACK PURPOSE

Being clear on feedback purpose brings greater intention and effectiveness to your feedback conversations, enabling you to better manage performance and support career development for your people.

Depending on what you identify, your Headline will be impacted.

As a quick refresher, there are three feedback purposes:

- **Instance**: Your goal is to share an observation of something that's happened.

- **Pattern**: You're deliberately shifting from, *"This happened again"* to, *"There's a pattern to address."*

- **Role Fit**: Your objective is an open and honest dialogue about the extent to which they're a fit for the role.

Instance conversations won't change your Headline, Pattern and Role Fit will.

When it's a Pattern, you literally want to use the word *pattern*. Here's a sampling of how you might use the word:

- I'd love to dive into a pattern I'm noticing within stakeholder management.

- There's a pattern I'm seeing that I worry will hold you back from being as successful as you want to be.

- I want to get curious about a pattern I've observed within your reporting.

When you're working with a team member who is struggling with their performance or a high performer with a tendency that could slow their career progression, Pattern conversations are the unspoken key to a manager's success. They enable you to better help them understand what and how to make the necessary changes to strengthen their growth and results.

When you determine that the feedback purpose is a Role Fit conversation, you also fold it into the Headline. That might sound like this:

Headline

For our one-to-one meeting today, I want to have an open and honest conversation about your ability to be successful in this role. Are you willing to dive in and have a candid conversation about where we go from here?

Once you're clear on the feedback purpose, it's time to identify the topic to be discussed.

HEADLINE STEP 2:
IDENTIFY NAME IT TO TAME IT

You will not tame what you can not name.

I won't sugar coat it; this skill is one of the hardest. It's also what ensures mutual understanding of the topic at hand.

The crux of it is this: you need to translate the narrative in your mind into one to three *neutral* words or phrases that encapsulate what you want to address.

The best way to learn this skill is to practice it. Let's run through two real scenarios.

Scenario #1

You have a team member who went on vacation and didn't think to set up an out of office message for clients. When they returned, they somehow let two client requests slip through the cracks. You regularly find that when you try to convey directions for something, they don't quite get it, and it takes them a long time to execute.

What might be some Name It to Tame Its in this scenario?

Below are some potential options for neutral words or phrases:

- **Urgency**: You're needing and wanting them to react more quickly.

- **Attention to detail**: Requests slipping and not thinking about details is harmful in client services.

- **Engagement**: Are they invested in succeeding in their role?

Notice these are neutral. We're not saying *lack* of urgency or *lack* of engagement. Keeping it neutral helps moderate how quickly the wall of defensiveness might shoot up.

Scenario #2

You have a team member who is a high performer, and previous managers have shied away from giving feedback to them because they get super defensive. This team member can be disruptive in team meetings and push back in a way that's not appropriate and borders on unprofessional. You need them to be able to receive feedback more gracefully and to harness their negativity with change in a different way.

What might be some Name It to Tame Its in this scenario?

Below are some considerations:

- **Adaptability**: You're needing them to be more adaptable to change.

- **Leadership presence**: They're seen as a leader due to performance, and now you need to shape how they show up and the impact of their presence.

- **Openness**: They appear closed off to feedback, and increasing their openness would help them and the team.

As you can see, there's no right or wrong necessarily.

To succeed with this tactic, say your scenario out loud, and then write down potential Name It to Tame It options.

Then ask yourself this question: *If I saw a 10% improvement in ____ (Name It to Tame It), would that meaningfully impact the situation?*

If the answer is yes, you're onto it. If the answer is no, keep playing with it.

Common Name It to Tame Its:

- Stakeholder management

- Performance consistency

- Client communication

- Change resilience

- Strategic planning

- Attention to detail

- Communication

- Decision-making

- Independence

- Collaboration

- Prioritization

- Adaptability

- Ownership

- Teamwork

- Urgency

Once you've identified what you're Naming, you're ready to craft your Transition.

If you're struggling to zero in on the behavior or performance you're wanting to name, in Chapter 18 I model an example of using an AI chatbot like Claude as a sounding board to brainstorm potential words or phrases for your situation.

HEADLINE STEP 3: CRAFT TRANSITION STATEMENT

The Transition component of your Headline is the difference between the person staying open and receptive or shutting down and raising their wall of defensiveness.

A strong Transition has three elements:

1. **Lean into their self-interest.** They'll be more likely to take action because they want to, rather than because you want them to.

2. **Send a message of your good intent.** This is you keeping the Relationship a priority, sending a message of trust and safety with your words and body language.

3. **Ask for permission.** We want to be respectful of their time and headspace. They might be running out the door for school pick up or battling a migraine, so give them permission to name another time if now doesn't work.

Now you put it all together to create your Headline.

Purpose + Name It to Tame It + Transition = Headline

The actual order does not matter, as you'll see below. It's about ensuring you've included the right components.

These Headlines tap into their self-interest, send messages of support and positive intent, ask permission, and then have clear Name It to Tame It (bolded) and Purpose where relevant:

- Can we connect for a few minutes? I'm seeing an opportunity to strengthen a pattern in your **communication**, and I want to help you excel further with your impact.

- I'd like to give you coaching in an area I know will be important for where you want to take your career. Do you have a few minutes to dive into **stakeholder relationships**?

- I'm seeing a pattern and opportunity to elevate your impact within the team. Can we hop on a quick call and explore? The topic I want to chat through is **role ownership**.

- I'm hoping you and I can connect on something I'm seeing as a potential blind spot, and it's on the topic of **collaboration**. Could we pop into a room and chat?

I want to call special attention to the last one.

This was used on me by my former leader, Jami.

She pulled me into the large conference room on the eighth floor of Yelp's office at the corner of Mission and 3rd in San Francisco.

She said to me, *"I want to shine a light on something I believe to be a blind spot for you. It's the way you're passive aggressive when you work with Susan."*

First of all, I was shocked. How did she know? I thought I was holding it together, but yes, this person was particularly challenging for me to work with and brought out some of my less-than-desirable qualities.

Secondly, as a person who has a natural tendency to be defensive, I didn't feel defensive about her message. It truly felt like I was getting the benefit of the doubt and that she was raising this out of care for my overall growth and role within the department.

Using this concept of a *"blind spot"* or a *"potential blind spot"* can be incredibly powerful when addressing more difficult behaviors.

OBSERVATION

Next in our Headline, Observation, Ask (HOA) framework is articulating what's been observed, experienced, and witnessed.

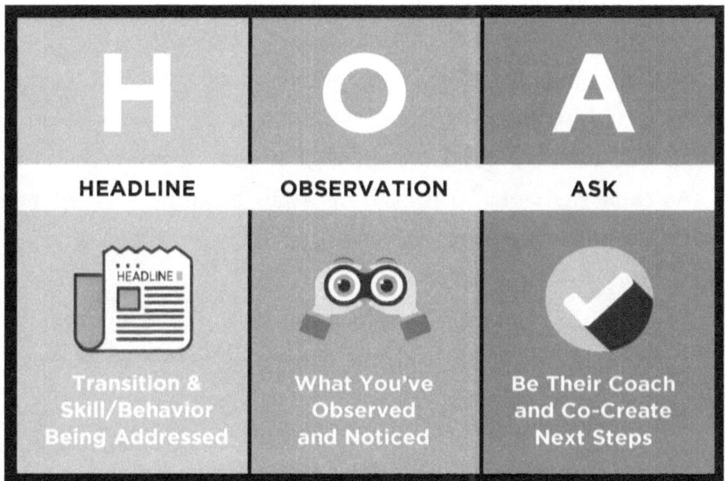

Your goal here is to objectively communicate the behavior or impact of the behavior as clearly and directly (with care) as possible.

My use of the word *objectively* is critical.

Consider this comparison:

- I feel like you're not engaged in your role. vs

- I've noticed a difference in your engagement lately.

Or how about the difference here:

- It felt like you got defensive when finance pushed back on your request.

- I saw a change in your tone and demeanor when finance pushed back on your request.

In each of these samples, the first was subjective, and the second was objective.

Sharing subjectively in a feedback conversation is a quick way to step into an emotional reaction pothole. They'll respond with something like, *"That's not how I felt,"* or, *"That's just how you feel."*

Sharing objectively—using *I noticed, I saw, I observed, I experienced,* or *I was made aware of*—is a lot harder to debate and can moderate how quickly their wall of defensiveness goes up.

As their manager, you observe a fair amount of their behavior. You also are sometimes put in the position of sharing feedback you didn't witness.

I'll specifically address how to share secondhand feedback in Chapter 5. For now I'll continue equipping you with addressing firsthand observations.

PERCEPTION VS. INTENTION

The most powerful concept within Observation that I can recommend is this: Perception vs. Intention.

It's the idea of sharing a more difficult observed behavior by way of extending the benefit of the doubt to them.

Think about situations where your people have been perceived as one of the following:

- Defensive

- Argumentative

- Condescending

- Poor collaborators

Imagine you'd approached them with this:

Observation

I noticed you used aggressive language with ops earlier today on chat. They gave you the resolution on the exception request and your response didn't convey an attitude of collaboration.

Now here's the same situation but using the Perception vs. Intention strategy. Notice what feels different.

Headline

I'm seeing something that has potential to hold you back from being as influential as you want to be. Can we connect for a few minutes on communication across teams?

Observation

I noticed in the chat thread earlier with ops that you used more aggressive language than you tend to use. I know it certainly wasn't your intention, and because I care about your growth and impact here, I want to get curious with you about what went down and what to adjust next time.

What differences in reaction would you imagine getting between these two approaches to sharing the Observation? Both call out more aggressive language being observed. One offers the benefit of the doubt. The other doesn't.

When we operate at the intersection of Mindset (assuming good intentions), Relationship (extending grace), and Delivery (communicating kindly and clearly), we will fearlessly deliver feedback.

ASK

Feedback without action is simply criticism.

A feedback conversation that doesn't identify *how* to do things differently moving forward leaves people feeling attacked, not invested in.

I was working with a client who came to me with a great deal of frustration. I'm guessing you're going to be able to relate.

Her leader told her that she needs to improve her executive presence if she wants to get promoted.

So I got curious with her:

- What about your executive presence has room for growth?

- What will an improvement in executive presence look and feel like?

- What do you want to work on versus what do you think your leader wants you to work on?

The punchline: she couldn't answer these questions.

She was deflated and discouraged. She'd received this "feed-back" and didn't know how to take action, or what within executive presence to prioritize developing.

Feedback without action is simply criticism.

That said, as the manager your job is not to have all the answers before going into the conversation.

You should have an idea of what improvement will look and feel like. You do not need to have an action plan.

It's during the Ask part of the framework that you shift into Coach Mode. What do coaches do?

- **Listen to what's being said and not said.** They listen between the lines.

- **Believe in you.** They catch you when you fall and then propel you forward.

- **Create space for discovery and creativity.** They empower exploration.

- **Lean into questions.** They ask more than they tell.

When you coach your people, you end up co-creating solutions. You're solving it *with* them, not *for* them.

There are two reasons for this:

- People are more likely to take action on something they created.

- What worked for you might not work for them.

Check out this example from a manager I was working with. Their team member was very inconsistent, one month hitting all their calls and metrics, the next month missing the basics. At times, the manager felt like they were lazy and just there to collect a paycheck.

This manager also had to resist the urge to *tell* this person exactly what to do. To increase the probability of them taking action, they need to have skin in the game. It's also a heck of a lot easier to hold someone accountable to an action they identified for themselves than one you told them to take.

Read through the language for this feedback conversation, and notice what stands out to you about the Ask.

Headline

I'm hoping you and I can connect on an opportunity to strengthen your consistency and set you up to thrive further in your role. Do you have a few minutes?

Observation

I've been noticing a pattern with your calls and performance. You'll hit the minimum one month and then have a month like August where you show solid performance. I want to talk about adjustments and improvements within your processes to enable you to deliver those great August results more consistently, setting you up for greater impact and stronger paychecks.

Ask

What's on your mind for what adjustments you'd want to make to empower yourself to succeed?

[Listen and encourage problem-solving.]

When unexpected things come up that could throw you off your plan, what steps do you want to think about taking then?

[Listen and encourage continued brainstorming.]

What else do you find helps you with consistency?

[Listen and encourage self-reflection.]

What actions do you want to put in place starting to-day?

[Listen and chime in with ideas as needed.]

What support would you like from me as you get going on these steps? What feels like the right cadence for us to revisit how these adjustments are panning out?

I hope the following stood out to you reading the example above:

- You're coaching them to their solutions.

- You're using "you" not "we" language.

- You're offering support after ideas and actions are discussed.

- You're asking about cadence of follow-up, setting the stage for accountability.

Increase clarity and alignment, and you'll positively impact behavior change.

COMMON MANAGER QUESTION

If you're thinking, *"What if I ask and they don't know?"* you are not alone.

The short answer: it's a trap, so don't fall for it.

The dreaded three words that move managers out of coaching-mode and into telling-mode: *"I don't know."*

When you take *"I don't know"* at face value, you're more likely to jump in with solutions, recommendations, and suggested next steps.

You limit their empowerment and strengthen their dependency on you.

There are three primary reasons they're holding back. *"I don't know"* can be code for the following:

- I'm not confident enough in my response.

- I'm afraid of what you're going to think of my solution.

- You might micromanage me and tell me what to do anyway, so why bother telling you what I think?

The next time you hear *"I don't know,"* try this:

1. Pause and acknowledge the challenge.

   No worries. Let's pause here for a moment. It's fair you likely weren't prepared to answer that question.

2. Then, welcome their creativity.

   Pretend for a moment you did have an idea for an initial next step. What might come to mind?

3. Then, stay silent. Let them think. They're going to say something like this:

   I guess what I could do is . . .

4. Jump on it. This is your chance to boost their confidence.

   Yes! Fantastic. Now build upon it. What else is now coming to mind?

5. Let them share, and applaud their thinking.

> *I like it. I trust you to get going with these next steps. I also knew that you had the answers in you all along. Don't be afraid to trust yourself.*

There is one important caveat.

When you have someone brand new in the role or brand new in the organization, you're going to need to consider when they truly don't know because they're new versus when they're needing affirmation of their thinking to boost their confidence.

When folks truly are stumped, they come to me differently. It sounds like this:

- I've been racking my brain, and I'm needing your help because I'm coming up blank.

- I'm feeling stumped as every solution I'm coming up with feels like the wrong path. I don't know what to do here. Can you help?

Be their coach, pose thoughtful questions, and you'll co-create actions that can enable their progress and growth.

CHAPTER SUMMARY

Delivery is an important component to creating a healthy feedback interaction and ultimately a vibrant feedback culture within your team.

Headline, Observation, Ask is a framework that creates a deliberate opening, minimizes your chances for overtalking, and ensures your feedback becomes actionable.

Below are your keys to success:

- **Headline**: Identify the type of feedback, know what to Name It, and transition in a way that focuses on their self-interest.

- **Observation**: Stay rooted in what's been seen, observed, and experienced, and for more difficult behaviors, consider perception vs. intention.

- **Ask**: Remember you're not telling them how to take action; you're co-creating action steps by being their coach.

SECONDHAND DELIVERY

A stakeholder has approached you with feedback about your team member. What do you do?

Do you share the feedback with them? But how? You weren't there. And how do you do it in a way that doesn't make them feel like they're being talked about?

These situations are loaded and challenging.

Let's make them easier for you.

IS IT VALUABLE?

Not all feedback is meant to be passed along.

Your first job is to discern the extent to which the action or behavior should be addressed.

Below are some filters you can use to discern whether to share or hold off:

- **Perception and reputation**: To what extent does this action or behavior have the ability to impact how the person is perceived within the business?

- **Timeliness and relevance**: How recent was this observed behavior, and is it still relevant?

- **Goal alignment**: To what extent does this feedback align with their growth goals?

If the feedback is personal preference, a narrowly held opinion, and/or not a barrier to their ability to be successful moving forward, you can opt to receive it gracefully without passing it along.

If you're unsure, get curious with the feedback provider. Seek to better understand the following:

- the severity of the action or behavior

- their perceived urgency

- the impact of the action or behavior

So often, I've found other leaders have brought me feedback more as a heads-up, not necessarily something that merits action. It's your job to discern whether you should share.

HOW TO POSITION

My goal in these scenarios is simple: help my team member gain valuable insight without feeling attacked.

The way I tend to bring it up is using language like the following:

- It's been shared with me . . .

- I've been looped in on . . .

- I was given a heads-up . . .

Let's take a look at a situation I had.

A stakeholder approached me with concerns about how my team member was prioritizing work for their org. We were in a matrix structure. Each of the learning and development professionals on my team directly supported different business units across the company.

My urgency and partnership with this stakeholder was vital for the dynamics of this matrix structure. First, I had to consider whether the feedback purpose was Instance, Pattern, or Role Fit. I decided to approach it as an Instance because a) this wasn't a firsthand observation, so b) I didn't know whether it was a Pattern. I decided to give the benefit of the doubt and approach as an Instance.

To get my Mindset right, I considered, *"Would I be holding back their growth if I didn't explore this with them?"* The answer was yes, and I decided the feedback was valuable to share.

Take note of what stands out in the following example, and then use that to compare to what I share below as deliberate word choices.

Headline

I'm hoping to connect on a way for you to have greater impact with your stakeholders, and the topic is prioritization. Do you have a few minutes?

Observation

I was given a heads-up that some outside projects have landed on your plate, creating a worry and perception that you're distracted from your core priorities. Because I know that's not your intention, and you're wanting to be effective with your partners, I wanted to shine a light on this and get curious with you.

Ask

Are you down to sort through your work and see what prioritization choices could be contributing to this perception?

[Listen for their experience, and pivot into coaching.]

Awesome. I'd propose our goal is to identify a way for you to take on these energizing side projects while ensuring your stakeholders are feeling they're getting everything they need.

[They signal agreement.]

Great, let's dive in and get you repositioned to kicking butt and taking names!

[Continue coaching to help them come up with a game plan.]

Let me call out a few things about the above language.

Headline

I'm focusing on their self-interest (their desire to have an impact), not the potential error in judgment or the disappointment the stakeholder shared with me.

Observation

I'm leveraging the power of perception vs. intention. I used this to communicate an important observation while reducing the risk of a larger reaction. By communicating that I'm assuming it wasn't their intention, I'm keeping them open. For this to work, you need to believe they had good intentions.

Ask

Feedback conversations should evolve into coaching interactions: collaborative conversations that enable future-focused troubleshooting. Notice that I don't ask what happened or why they made certain choices. I'm less interested in what didn't go well and more interested in what might be more impactful moving forward.

COMMON MANAGER QUESTIONS

WHAT IF THEY WANT TO KNOW WHO TOLD ME?

I'd respond by helping them zoom out on the opportunity, rather than zooming in on who was the informant. Continuing from the scenario above, it might sound like this:

I can appreciate the curiosity. This is less about who is looking out for your work and more about an opportunity to zoom out and reflect on what priorities might inadvertently be competing and reducing your impact in your core work. Let's take a look at everything on your plate and get you set up for sustained impact.

WHAT IF THEY'RE WANTING EXAMPLES? DO I LIST THEM OUT?

This can be a conversational trap. They ask for examples, so you give an example. They give an explanation, so you give another example . . . and so on. Soon you're in a tennis match: point, counter point. Not productive.

If this happened for the above example, I'd respond with this:

Let's pause here. Tell me more about what's running through your mind.

[You're now inviting explanations, but you're also giving them space to express confusion, frustration, etc.]

That's fair. I can appreciate you're feeling surprised and like you're being criticized for helping someone else with another project.

What's more powerful than listing examples is to connect back to the feeling of a competing priority. Can you tap back into recent moments when you've prioritized another project over your deliverables for primary stakeholders?

[They typically can.]

Great, now let's pivot into thinking about what you can do differently next time, so you're prioritizing core deliverables while still feeling energized by these side projects.

CHAPTER SUMMARY

Secondhand feedback doesn't have to create awkwardness or defensiveness.

When you filter for what's truly valuable, position it with care, assume good intent, and use a simple structure to guide the conversation, you turn a potential *"someone's talking about me"* moment into an opportunity for growth.

That's how you move from being a messenger to being a coach who equips your team to have greater impact.

FEARLESS FEEDBACK FRAMEWORK SAMPLE SITUATIONS

Now that you've gotten a breakdown of the framework, view this chapter as the chapter you will flip back to again and again as you seek sample language and inspiration for your situations.

I've provided many real examples of feedback conversations, divided by conversation type: Instance, Pattern, and Role Fit.

Some language you'll read and instantly feel inspired to use yourself. Others you'll feel the sentiment and want to wordsmith to your style. Use this language. Improve this language. Make it your own.

As you're reading through and thinking, *"Hmm, what should*

I do if they push back or react," have no fear. Chapter 7 covers how to handle reactions, and Chapter 8 provides additional sample situations that show how to address reactions.

Here's a quick glimpse of the topics in the following examples.

- Instance (Examples #1 and #2)

- Pattern (Examples #3 and #4)

- Role Fit (Examples #5 and #6)

INSTANCE FEEDBACK SITUATIONS

One way to make your life easier is to think High Cadence, Low Stakes.

When you share tidbits and real-time suggestions that incrementally elevate the work and impact of your people, a few things happen. First, your relationship (and their performance) strengthens because you're engaging more with them, and they feel your investment in their career development.

This is validated by Gallup: "Employees are 3.6x more likely to strongly agree that they are motivated to do outstanding work when their manager provides daily (vs. annual) feedback.[5]"

Secondly, your mindset strengthens because feedback with this person begins to feel less daunting.

Consider the alternative: we don't share coaching and feedback at a regular enough cadence, so when we do need to give feedback, it feels like a higher-stakes interaction.

---

5 Denise McLain and Bailey Nelson, "How Effective Feedback Fuels Performance," Gallup, 2024.

Higher stakes means greater stress and more of a chance for inner narratives to take over, so the probability of putting off the conversation goes up dramatically.

Adopting the High Cadence, Low Stakes mentality starts with committing to addressing things when they're in the Instance stage, before they've become Patterns.

INSTANCE EXAMPLE 1

I had a team member who I was training to take on advanced admin work within our beast of a learning management system (LMS). Being thorough with details impacted how and where employee training content was displayed, not to mention who got assigned the training paths. Accuracy with the finer details mattered.

They were working on deploying a high visibility program within our LMS and I found multiple basic errors. Making mistakes was not their norm and I wanted to address the situation before any more racked up. I had (and still have) a great relationship with them. I approached with a *"no biggie"* perspective to put them at ease and focus on the objective: ensuring mistakes don't continue to happen.

Headline

Hey friend . . . can we connect to help make your work within our LMS easier? The high-level topic I want to chat through is attention to detail. Do you have five minutes now, or would later be better?

Observation

I checked out the setup for the admin properties for the expansion project and noticed you missed a couple. Because that's not typically like you, I thought it was worth connecting.

Ask

> *Can we take a look together and then pivot to ensuring you're off to the races moving forward? You're typically super in tune to details. What's feeling different here?*
>
> [Listen and hold space. They share that they've been doing this work while multitasking in meetings.]
>
> *Aaahhh . . . that makes a bit more sense as to what was behind these uncommon errors. That said, seeing as being mildly distracted has created errors, what are you thinking you want to approach differently moving forward?*
>
> [Listen and support. They identify they need to do this detailed work when they have focused time.]
>
> *Good thinking. Doing this work when not multitasking is a good call.*
> *What can I do on my end to support your efforts now that we've pinpointed the root issue?*

Mistakes happen. Not calling attention to the out-of-character performance would have been a miss on my part.

Where this conversation ultimately continued was into an exploration of being overwhelmed enough that they felt their only option was to multitask in meetings. What initially presents as one feedback opportunity often opens the door to a deeper conversation about surrounding factors.

INSTANCE EXAMPLE 2

What I'm about to share comes from a video of me modeling HOA with a former team member of mine. The situation we're modeling was of having just come out of a meeting in which Pat was defensive when working with a cross functional team.

This is a type of behavior that I absolutely don't want to see turn into a Pattern, and I hold myself to addressing asap, while it's an Instance.

Below you can read the core points of the message delivered.

To see how this conversation moves from text on a page to a human-to-human interaction, visit www.fearlessfeedbackbook.com/resources. In just a four-minute video, you'll see warmth, care, and directness in the delivery.

As you read through, consider underlining the words or phrases that feel most impactful.

Headline

Hey Pat! Thanks so much for staying back from our team meeting. The reason I wanted to connect with you for a few minutes is I'm noticing something that has the possibility of holding you back from being as successful as you want to be. It's on the topic of defensiveness.

Observation

In our meeting a few minutes ago, I noticed this defensiveness come up. You had an idea and presented your solution, and some folks had follow-up questions. What I noticed was your wall went up a bit, and you weren't the open and curious person that I often know you to be. I wanted to bring this to your attention because I want to set you up for success.

Ask

And first, I want to ask you . . . can you relate to that feeling when you felt your defensiveness come up?

[Listen for what he's feeling with what's on his plate, and acknowledge the moment getting the better of him. Then continue to encourage and support.]

What would be most helpful as you identify those moments and need small course corrections in the moment?

[Listen and encourage reflection and brainstorming.]

My commitment to you is, in real time, to help you build that muscle of staying curious and collaborative.

Might we create a code word, that only you and I know, so that during meetings, I can gently redirect you if I see your wall of defensiveness start to build. That can be your signal to pivot until you begin to hone in on this yourself.

[Confirm alignment on action created.]

Thank you so much for your openness and willingness to hear this coaching.

Real-time behavioral feedback is the most challenging but has the greatest impact on team dynamics and performance.

Sometimes helping someone to build self-awareness is the first step. In this example, he knew what not to do (get defensive); his challenge was having self-awareness when it was happening.

Creating simple systems, flags, or code words can be a useful tool when they know what to do, they're just needing help recognizing it in the moment.

What stood out to you with the wording and phrasing choices made in this example? What could you leverage in your own style?

PATTERN FEEDBACK SITUATIONS

These next examples illustrate addressing patterns of performance and behavior that need to get turned around. By using the word *pattern* in our communication, we send an important message of urgency: that action does need to be taken.

You're also going to get introduced to Pattern's cousin, Cycle. There are times in which we can strengthen our message by the naming of a cycle. As you'll see in the first example, naming a cycle in their performance can help to connect the dots or help to illustrate something they might not be aware is happening. And the increased awareness and clarity of message will help you to help them break the cycle.

PATTERN EXAMPLE 3

What do you do when someone on your team is inconsistent? They cruise and fall back; you address it, and then they do great work. Rinse and repeat.

It's not just a Pattern; it's a Cycle. Naming it is key to creating the change you want to see. This is performance management in action.

In this scenario, we've got a manager who was a bit at her wits' end, feeling like she was having Groundhog Day conversations. She couldn't figure out why her team member demonstrated bursts of output and productivity after each conversation they had about performance before falling back into the same behaviors.

As this manager and I discussed the challenge, it became clear that the issue was a Cycle, and the Name It to Tame It she settled on was *performance consistency*, a neutral, accurate descriptor of what she was addressing.

Here's the sample language you can also use if this situation rings true in your management journey.

Headline

I'm hoping to connect today on a cycle I'm noticing that is likely to get in the way of where you want to take your career. Do you have a few minutes to talk about performance consistency?

Observation

Here's what I'm noticing, and I'm going to be curious about the extent to which you can feel and identify what I'm see-ing. The cycle I'm observing goes like this: you'll be in a slower spot, we'll connect and chat about performance and output, you'll have a burst of creativity and outcomes, and then performance fades back. I'm invested in helping you to break this cycle to demonstrate more consistent performance, so you can continue reaching the next levels within your role and the org.

Ask

Let me pause here. Reflecting on the last couple of months, can you identify these ups and downs I'm shining a light on?

[Listen and encourage self-reflection.]

Thinking of those times when you're firing on all cylin-ders, what can you identify that helps you and your pro-duction?

[Listen and remain genuinely curious in coaching mode. You're not solving it for them, you're solving it with them.]

Now go to the other end when you can plateau and pe-ter out a bit. What's at play during those times?

[Listen and help them build on their insights.]

Okay, so we've looked at both ends of the spectrum, the highs and the lows. Now we need to play a bit of Gold-ilocks and find the just-right. What do you want to start thinking about adjusting, so you're breaking this cycle and being more consistent with performance?

[Listen and encourage action identification.]

Great, and what else?

[Listen and support as they create their own action plan.]

As you get going with these actions, what support would you like from me? And at what cadence does it make sense for us to touch base on how you're doing with these new habits?

If you want to increase the probability that your feedback conversation results in changed performance and behavior, you need to be the coach who is willing to be appropriately persistent.

The above example could have easily ended with the team member hearing the feedback and showing tacit agreement. That's what most managers would do.

You're not most managers.

Notice how many coaching questions were posed within Ask. Your job is to push ever so slightly with care and support to challenge them and get them to make their own commitments. Then you can offer support and create alignment on how you two will continue to monitor progress in this area.

The difference between good and great lies in the willingness to get uncomfortable.

Appropriately challenging our people is uncomfortable at first, and then it becomes the spark that keeps the fire within the team going.

PATTERN EXAMPLE 4

This is one of the more common and frustrating conversations I witness managers wanting to address with their people. Rather than using a specific case study, let me model some sample language you can consider the next time you're wanting to address independence with a team member.

First, how does this conversation typically present itself? It typically starts with seeing behaviors such as a team member being passive, wanting your input on everything, or being more reactive than proactive.

It's also highly probable that you're starting to feel like you're hand-holding too much.

Second, I wouldn't be covering all our bases if I didn't highlight another contributing factor in these cases.

Yes, there are team members who have hit the expiration date for hand-holding in their role, despite your best efforts to encourage them to think and act on their own.

There are also cases where some of your actions might be inadvertently creating so much of a backstop that whatever independent, proactive thinking and acting they might have had has been reduced because they always know you've got their back and you'll jump in to fill any gaps.

Prior to a thoughtful conversation about independence, be sure you reflect on how you could be creating so much of a safety net that they don't step into their empowerment.

I'll note one last thing about the following model language: I used this with a group of managers for a live training for a Fortune 500 company. When we crafted the Observation portion, I noticed the London office (who was on mute) started to laugh and engage in side chatter.

Being curious, I invited London to come off mute and share what was funny.

Their response was: *"Katie, it's like you know exactly who I'm managing right now!"*

Needless to say, laughter ensued, and every manager walked away feeling better equipped to address one of their more frustrating situations.

Headline

I'm seeing an opportunity for you to have greater impact within this team, and given how invested you are in your growth, I'm wondering if you have a few minutes to talk about independence within your role.

Observation

I've been noticing a pattern that is going to hold you back from being as successful as you're hoping. It's a passive pattern of waiting for direction. For you to grow further in this role, I'd like to see you step into greater independence and ownership of your work and your role, seeking less of my direction and creating and proposing your own path and strategy.

Ask

I can appreciate "independence" and "ownership" might feel a bit murky. Let's chat through what that means because we've got a great opportunity for you to stand more firmly in what I know you're capable of.

Would you be game to talk it through so you can feel truly empowered to be more independent with your work?

[They typically say yes and are eager at this point because I've yet to meet someone who doesn't want independence, autonomy, and ownership of their work and role. Put on your coaching hat and get curious with them, all with an intended outcome that they know what actions they can take to step into improved independence.]

Below are coaching questions that could help:

- What does greater independence look and feel like to you?

- Imagining you felt empowered to make more decisions in your role, what decisions would you start making?

- What's one thing I could start doing to help support your greater independence?

- What's one thing I could do differently, so I'm not inadvertently in your way?

Pause here and reflect. What other coaching questions could you leverage to create clarity, alignment, action, and support? Write them down, have them ready for the next time you're addressing independence and ownership.

ROLE FIT FEEDBACK SITUATIONS

Role Fit conversations are an interesting blend of challenging and liberating. These conversations come after you've been having Pattern conversations related to their performance or behavior, and you're not seeing the improvement you, their stakeholders, and the business are needing.

In the context of critical feedback scenarios, I view these as conversations to have before moving to a Performance Improvement Plan (PIP). I want to give them an opportunity to truly have an open and honest conversation about how they're feeling in the role.

Role Fit conversations also require us to truly step into the Fearless Feedback Framework. We need to operate at a solid intersection of a caring Mindset, leading with safety in the Relationship, and appropriate directness with our Delivery.

As you read these examples, write down your questions. I

invite you to reach out with your curiosities (katie@endur-anceboss.com).

ROLE FIT EXAMPLE 5

This one is a tricky one. The employee was new and in their probationary period. Compared to what was typically seen from new hires—eagerness to learn, focus, good questions, commitment to excelling in the probationary period—this employee had a lackadaisical approach, wasn't taking initiative to learn the role, and was often on her phone rather than engaging while folks were trying to mentor her. A decision needed to be made about retaining her, and because we never want someone to be surprised when they're let go due to performance, a conversation needed to be had.

Headline

Thank you for making time to meet with me. I want to use today to have an open and honest conversation as I have concerns about your ability to be successful in this role. There are two categories I want to look at: one is professionalism, and second is knowledge retention.

Observation

Let me go ahead and start with knowledge retention. I will be candid in saying that I have observed that even when I have given you the opportunity to dive into resources, to find answers to some of the basic elements of the role, I'm a bit disappointed that you struggle to identify and retain the answers. We're going to want to think about what actions you want to take that will enable you to boost your knowledge retention.

Then the second category I want to address is professionalism. I've observed that when you're working with Valerie, you're on your phone. The staff and patients in this office aren't going to take you seriously seeing you texting so much. (You can say this with warmth and a smile.)

I wouldn't be doing right by you if I didn't shine a light on this because I believe it's a blind spot for you. You may not be aware that this is creating a perception that you're potentially less serious or less invested in this position.

And I don't believe that's your intention.

Ask

So let me pause here. Those are two categories of concern, all under the umbrella of wanting you to succeed through your probationary period.

Which one do we want to dive into first in terms of the actions you want to commit to, so that you can make progress and demonstrate to us you can be successful in this role?

All feedback conversations, especially those focused on role fit or concern, should be a dialogue, not a monologue delivered by the manager.

That's why, for this example, we want to ask which topic of concern they want to tackle first and then get curious with them and focus on gaining commitments.

Here's where I would take the coaching and commitments in this situation:

- What's on your mind for how we'll know you're making progress in these areas?

- What shifts in your habits will you begin making?

- What additional support would you like from me?

- I'd propose we revisit progress two weeks from now. What touch points do you want to build in between now and then?

ROLE FIT EXAMPLE 6

This next example is more direct and models how these conversations can, and should, elevate in urgency when poor behaviors continue despite consistent sharing of feedback.

There's a particular phrase I want to highlight in this sample.

You'll notice in the Observation, there's a shift and the words, *"not engaging in the way I need you to,"* are used.

I typically stay away from conversations being about what *I*, or *the business*, needs of the person. I typically find the motivation to change is lower when someone wants us to do something versus when we feel it's in our best interest. That's why I take the intentional approach of making the conversation about their wellbeing, success, or future, and yes, the byproduct is I'm getting what I need from them as well.

When someone isn't implementing coaching and feedback at the Instance and Pattern levels, and you begin to worry about the extent to which they can succeed in the role and on the team, it's fair to shift to communicating what you (or the business) needs of them, as you'll see in this sample.

Headline

I'm hoping to connect with you on what's likely to be an uncomfortable topic. I'm having concerns about your ability to be successful in this role.

Observation

We've been talking about the need for problem-solving and positivity, and the reaction I witnessed from you with this morning's announcement of shifting roles and responsibilities was another example of you not engaging in the way I need you to.

Ask

We're approaching a crossroads, and I want to openly discuss where you are and what can be done to shift your trajectory because I want you to be happy and successful, whether here or elsewhere.

Things to then explore:

- What's your satisfaction here?

- What commitment do you want to make to more positively respond to changes?

- What will be different?

- What do you need from me to sustain this improvement?

CHAPTER SUMMARY

These examples not only model effective language, they are packed with nuances and tactics that will strengthen how you approach feedback.

Below are the techniques used in these examples:

- **High Cadence, Low Stakes**: Commit to a greater frequency of coaching, and watch and see how things don't feel as high stakes.

- **Pattern's cousin, Cycle**: Watch for cycles of performance and behaviors, another powerful example where word choice matters.

- **With vs. For**: Increase your probability of them taking action by solving with them, as opposed to for them.

- **Appropriate Persistence**: Push and challenge your people as great coaches do.

- **Pivoting from Their Self-Interest**: Know there's a time and place to pivot away from messaging that focuses on their self-interest and shifts to what you (and the business) need from them, but this is not our default approach.

RESPONDING TO REACTIONS

The fear of how someone may respond to feedback is a top reason managers put off the conversation.

You likely can relate. The dread of an angry reaction. The discomfort of someone crying. The annoyance of someone offering excuses rather than accountability.

On the flip side, with positive feedback, it's not uncommon for managers to worry that if they share too much positive reinforcement, the person will react by asking for a raise or promotion. The result? Putting off the sharing of feedback.

While everything you've learned thus far has been in the spirit of moderating the size and scope of the reaction to enable an impactful conversation, my goal is not to eliminate reactions in feedback conversations.

I want to see a level of emotion, curiosity, and investment when I share information that will help them be their best.

I'm frankly more concerned if someone doesn't have any response than someone who gets defensive or falls apart. If they don't react, I get curious about their investment in their growth, their role, and our team.

To boost your confidence and competence handling the full spectrum of emotional reactions, we lean into the Fearless Feedback Framework.

Mindset, Relationship, and Delivery all have key roles to play when emotions and reactions arise. Just as in the heart of the feedback conversation, the intersection of these three elements is also where you'll effectively be able to navigate their reaction.

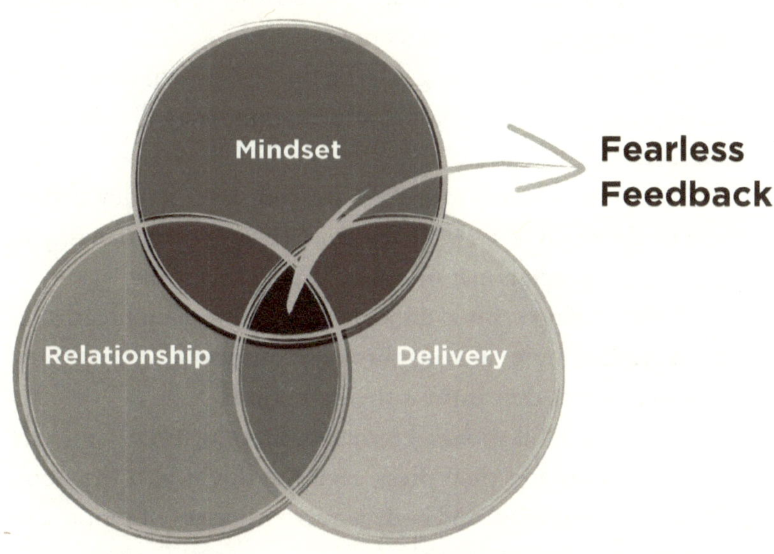

MINDSET FOR REACTIONS

You'll remember our three guiding principles that create a powerful foundation for our Mindset in feedback conversations:

1. Care deeply.

2. Hold a high bar.

3. Focus on strengths and energizing work.

These remain true when we're faced with navigating their thoughts and feelings about the feedback they've just received.

If you need additional tips to keep your Mindset in a productive place, leverage these additional pointers.

1. STAY CALM

Here's the uncomfortable truth: there's only room for one person to be emotional, and it's not you.

This is their time. You get to be the composed, caring, and direct manager who is sharing information that will help them succeed.

Even when your buttons get pushed, even if they accuse you of shortfalls, even if their excuses drive you bananas, you don't get to react in that moment. This is their time.

When staying calm is difficult, take a few deep breaths: in through your nose and out through your mouth. Do it three to four times as they express their emotions.

It's also helpful to stay grounded, literally. Press your feet into the floor, and then press each toe down into the floor. This gives your brain and body a micro moment of reprieve to help you not lose your cool.

2. STAY FOCUSED ON THE TASK AT HAND

You set out to have a conversation that will improve their success in their role. You have information to help them succeed.

When they shut down, go silent, cry, or even offer excuses and get angry, you still have a job to do. Stay focused on the task at hand.

In the moment, when you feel your mind wanting to abandon and give up, reach for the closest piece of paper, and quickly write a word or two about what's important about helping them in this area.

Maybe you write one of these:

- Growth

- Impact

- Legacy

- Teamwork

The mini moment can help you remember why you're here and keep you in the Mindset that will serve their performance and development. Growth lives on the other side of discomfort.

3. DON'T TAKE THE REACTION AT FACE VALUE

When I was twenty-two, my manager, Bridget, gave me feedback that forever changed how I view reactions to feedback.

We were working at SCORE! Educational Centers in the Corte Madera Town Center in Northern California. She pulled me into the all-glass conference room with a red boomerang table.

She said, *"Katie, I want to give you feedback that the other directors in the center feel like you get defensive every time they try to offer a suggestion."*

I swear to you, these were the exact next words out of my mouth, *"No I don't!"*

Case in point, I suppose.

But here's the deal. In that moment, Bridget would have

described my reaction as defensive. After all, I immediately denied it. That was the external display of emotion.

Let me tell you what was happening inside.

I was embarrassed. I was disappointed in myself. I'd been a high achiever, straight-A kinda kid who never got in trouble. At that moment I felt like I'd failed because she'd had to tell me that I wasn't knocking it out of the park.

My internal experience was *very* different from my external display of emotion.

I share this because we cannot fall into the trap of making assumptions about the emotion we see.

Here's another quick story to illustrate.

There was a woman named Colleen in my feedback training course. When we got into a discussion about internal versus external display of emotion when receiving feedback, she shared this:

> *Oh yeah, I got feedback from my leader that I thought was totally bogus. What he saw was a smile and a nod. What I was doing inside was shooting daggers with my eyes. I was so furious!*

She quit that job soon after.

To successfully navigate reactions to feedback, we need a Mindset of not taking the reaction at face value. Instead, reframe to recognize this is a powerful place to get curious and a starting point that can bring your relationship closer.

RELATIONSHIP FOR REACTIONS

Your primary task within Relationship is to maintain genuine trust and preserve psychological safety throughout the interaction. Your demeanor and words need to create an environment in which they know they're safe and can trust you're focused on enabling their success.

You are not the bull in the china shop pointing out their flaws, nor are you blazing past their reaction and pretending it's not happening.

You are sharing feedback that makes them feel you're invested in their growth and helps them see a path forward, even in the toughest of situations.

Keeping their safety and care top of mind is essential, even when you're frustrated, or the conversation isn't going how you thought.

Practically speaking, this can mean taking some of the following actions:

- **Physical Positions**: If you're in-person for the conversation, physically sit on the same couch or next to them at the corner of the table. Avoid sitting directly across from them at a large table. This positioning can feel much more threatening.

- **Body Language**: Face your shoulders toward them, giving your full attention. Lean in and send a message of investment and commitment. Avoid crossing your arms or leaning back in your chair, either of which send a message of distance and mistrust.

- **Facial Expressions**: If you're on a video call, turn on your self-view to help you monitor your appearance of warmth and presence, particularly if you're someone who is very expressive with your face.

When done well, these moments have a true opportunity to strengthen your relationship.

DELIVERY FOR REACTIONS

What you say and how you say it absolutely matters in these moments.

Similar to how you learned HOA for the Delivery component of the feedback conversation, I have a complementary framework for how you can respond to their reaction.

First, there are two foundational best practices that enable the success of the framework you're about to learn.

BEST PRACTICE 1: DON'T PLAY TENNIS

This is what gets most managers.

It starts with a reaction from your team member like this:

- Who told you?

- What you're not factoring in is . . .

- Can you give me an example of when I did this?

- But I did that because first the other person said . . .

Then you feel compelled to respond. Next thing you know, you're in a point, counter-point interaction.

You both feel frustrated, they don't get the clarity and message they need, and you don't end up changing their performance or behavior.

Here's how you succeed: assume it's true.

You're not a detective, an investigator, or a litigator. You don't need to go get everyone else's side of the story. Remember, if a perception was created, you're dealing with impacting the perception, somewhat regardless of who is right, wrong, etc.

Here's how it can sound:

Them

But what they didn't tell you is that first I tried X, which didn't work. Then they did Y, and I couldn't do my end of the project because of Z.

Manager

Let's assume that's all true. What I'm not aiming to do is rehash and litigate the past. I am interested in setting you up for future impact. Assuming that's all true and knowing what you know, let's talk about some tactics for future You.

You're not playing tennis. You're not going point, counter-point. You are locked in on what's important: impacting their future performance and behaviors.

Here's why this is important:

- **Mindset**: You're staying focused on the task at hand, caring for their success, and holding a high bar.

- **Relationship**: You're reducing the feeling that they need to defend themselves, helping you maintain trust and safety.

- **Delivery**: Assuming it's true and refocusing to impact future decisions enables you to continue with your message and ultimately move back to coaching for action.

BEST PRACTICE 2: IT'S *AND,* NOT *OR*

We often think in terms of this or that, especially when worst-case assumptions have a grip on our Mindset.

In the context of feedback conversations, that can leave us having thoughts such as, *"They'll receive it well, or they'll hate me."*

This foundational element is about remembering the power of *and*. Two things can be true at the same time.

They can be upset *and* understand the need to change.

They can be emotional, *and* you can hold them accountable.

They can offer an explanation *and* get refocused to doing it differently next time.

You can be direct *and* care deeply for them.

You can challenge their thinking *and* hold space for vulnerability.

You can share a tough message *and* strengthen your relationship.

Living in the *and*, rather than the *or*, enables us to more effectively manage and lead humans. We are a messy and complex species; holding dualities helps us thrive.

As you continue through the rest of this chapter and read sample situations with reactions, notice when you see *and* (vs. *or*) in the word choices for Delivery. It's a key tool for managers that can positively impact the trajectory of the conversation.

HEAR FRAMEWORK

Now let's get down to brass tacks on what you're going to do (and say) when your feedback is met with a reaction.

Here's what this framework enables us to do: **help our people feel seen and heard while refocusing on action they can take moving forward.**

HEADLINE	EXPLORE	ACKNOWLEDGE	REFOCUS
Hear and articulate the individual's reaction in a nonjudgemental way	Get curious using neutral language to assess what's driving the reaction	Acknowledge and validate what you hear the person saying	Refocus on the heart of the feedback, focusing on the future, not the past
"I notice you've gotten quiet." "I'm seeing this is creating a reaction for you."	"What's running through your mind?" "Help me to better understand how to read your reaction."	"I can appreciate you're feeing caught off guard." "It's fair that you're surprised and worried about what others are thinking about you."	"What's something you want to do differently next time?" "What's an action you want to take to get things going?"

MODEL IN ACTION

Before I break down each component and highlight pitfalls and pro tips for mastery, below is a quick example of how it might sound.

Imagine someone on your team was working with a cross-functional partner and got a bit snarky in their communication. You got looped into the situation, and you're now sharing feedback about how they were perceived in that moment.

You've opened up with an intentional Headline and shared the Observation, and then you see their body language shift and their jaw clench before they go quiet.

Your point of recognizing a reaction, even as subtle as a change in body language, is your signal to jump over into the HEAR framework.

Hear

Let's pump the brakes here for a second. I'm noticing your body language changing, and I want to pause here and open up a safe space to dive into what might be feeling uncomfortable.

Explore

Tell me what's going through your mind.

[They let you know that the feedback is feeling one-sided because they did get snarky with another team but only after the other person was nonresponsive on a time-sensitive issue.]

Acknowledge

I can appreciate what you're saying about how they were engaging and behaving. I can also appreciate how frustrating that can feel.

Refocus

Recognizing they are important stakeholders of yours, and you'll need their help in the future, what's something you'd want to challenge yourself to do differently next time?

If you are also an audio/visual learner, visit www.fearless-feedbackbook.com/resources to listen and watch a six-minute demonstration of the HEAR model in action.

Reactions tend to surface after Observation and before we pivot into coach-mode with the Ask of our HOA framework although this is not a hard and fast rule. What remains true is wherever the reaction happens (after Observation, within or after Ask), you'll use HEAR and resume your coaching by diving back into Ask.

To illustrate, here's how they come together:

Now let's look at each step, so you can confidently adopt and leverage the next time you're facing a reaction.

STEP 1: HEAR

This step is about pausing the conversation and addressing what you're hearing and seeing in them.

Imagine the reaction is a mild speed bump on the road to your destination.

There you are, feeling like you're cruising along. Your Headline sent a message of care and investment and asked for permission to continue. You're progressing into Observation, and then they display an emotion. It's a speed bump.

If you were driving a car, you wouldn't just blow past. You'd slow down, recognize it's there, and intentionally travel across.

That's what we want to do when the reaction happens. It's our cue to slow down.

And the first thing you do is name it. Say what you see and hear in them.

Below are some examples of how that might sound:

- Let's pause here for a moment. I'm noticing that you've gotten a bit quiet.

- Let's take a quick moment. I want to honor that I'm hearing emotion in your voice, and I want to offer time and space for you to be heard.

- Let's pump the brakes here for a second. I'm seeing this is creating a reaction for you.

Naming what you're hearing and seeing is step 1. Now you need to get curious and give them the floor.

STEP 2: EXPLORE

Using neutral language, invite your team member to share what's running through their mind. In asking them to share more, you're also inviting them to share excuses and explanations, which is okay. It gives you more to work with when you shift back to coaching them.

Below are statements I like to use to explore their reaction:

- Talk to me about what's running through your mind.

- Help me to better understand how to read your reaction.

- Tell me more about the wheels that are spinning in your mind.

It's here that you then listen with patience, openness, and calmness. They might blame you for the situation. They might throw someone else under the bus. They might break down in tears of exhaustion.

Whatever it is, ensure that your body and face are sending a message of safety and care.

There's one pitfall to be aware of.

It's possible they resist, don't want to share, or say something like, *"No, nothing, just taking it all in."*

If your gut tells you that's not the full truth, address it head on.

With deep care, I will respond, *"With the greatest care and investment in you and your growth, I'm going to respectfully say that I don't believe you. Truly, I'm interested in hearing what's running through your mind."* I say this with a small, genuine smile, so I'm gently conveying my desire for them to truly be honest with me.

It's worked every single time I've had to use it.

After they've shared, it's time to validate and acknowledge how they're thinking and feeling.

STEP 3: **ACKNOWLEDGE**

It's the combination of Explore + Acknowledge that creates the feeling of being seen and heard.

Whatever they've shared with us, we can communicate true validation and appreciation for their thinking and feeling.

I tend to use phrases such as these:

- I can appreciate this has been a tough message to hear, and you're still processing.

- I can appreciate that you're feeling attacked, and your walls of defensiveness are rising.

- It's fair to feel surprised and worried about what this means for your reputation.

There's one phrase I don't use: *"It's okay."*

Here's why: I'm trying to change behavior. If my response is, *"It's okay,"* then I'm suggesting approval, which is counter to what I'm trying to do with this feedback interaction.

Instead, my focus is to validate and acknowledge how they're experiencing the moment.

STEP 4: **REFOCUS**

With validation for their experience, it's my job to Refocus back to the task at hand.

This feedback conversation started because there was a behavior or performance that should be changed. It's here that you live in the *and*.

They can feel frustrated, *and* there's still a pivot to make. They can have an explanation for their behavior, *and* they should still choose a different action next time.

Here's how the Refocus might sound:

- Knowing what you know now, what's something you'd want to tackle differently next time?

- Recognizing this likely won't be the last time a situation like this happens, what do you want to dive into first to get you set up for greater impact next time?

- Acknowledging how you're feeling and knowing it still remains true that you've got important work on your plate, what commitments do you want to make to yourself moving forward?

I'm hoping you're noticing something in this sample language.

Notice the use of *you* versus *we*.

Too often I find managers overuse *we* in feedback and performance conversations. *Here's what we can do, what we are going to do is . . . , etc.*

If you want someone to take accountability and ultimately take a different action, it's on them, not us, to make that happen.

They're in the driver's seat, and we're an active front seat passenger. We're there to help them navigate and stay focused on the road ahead. If they choose not to put their foot on the gas and not make progress in the way they'd want, we need to help them own that decision.

Your statement or question of Refocus is what brings you back into the Headline, Observation, Ask framework. Refocus opens the door to continue into Ask where you keep your coaching hat on, and you help coach them how to move forward.

The following chapter will model how our two frameworks come together to impactfully share feedback, address reactions, and then wrap up with action and alignment.

CHAPTER SUMMARY

The goal isn't that your people don't react; the goal is that when they do, you effectively help them to feel seen and heard. The Fearless Feedback Framework helps you strike this right balance.

- **Mindset**: Stay calm and focused on the task at hand. Don't take their reaction at face value.

- **Relationship**: Send deliberate messages of trust and safety with your physical presence, body language, and facial expressions.

- **Delivery**: Remember you're not in a tennis match, and these conversations are not binary. We get to operate in duality.

You will further compliment your Delivery by integrating the HEAR framework into your feedback delivery. When a reaction is displayed, pivot from Headline, Observation, Ask (HOA) into HEAR:

1. **Hear**: Pause and name what you're seeing or hearing in them.

2. **Explore**: Get curious and give them the floor to share their experience.

3. **Acknowledge**: Validate their experience and perspective.

4. **Refocus**: Zero in on one element of behavior or action to get back to the task at hand.

Leaning into Fearless Feedback while practicing the HEAR framework can improve how your feedback is received and implemented and ultimately strengthen your relationship dynamics.

FEARLESS FEEDBACK FRAMEWORK SAMPLE SITUATIONS WITH REACTIONS

Your Mindset is telling you that you have a valuable observation to help a team member do their best work.

You've invested in a strong foundational Relationship, and you've earned and maintained the trust of your people.

You're well positioned with thoughtful Delivery having dug into Headline, Observation, Ask.

And now you have the HEAR framework in your back pocket for addressing any reactions that come up during the conversation.

It's time to put them all together.

Similar to Chapter 6, this chapter lays out scenarios based on Instance, Pattern, and Role Fit. What you're now going to see is how Headline, Observation, Ask and HEAR come together to share feedback, address reactions, refocus on the feedback, and end with greater alignment and action.

Within each scenario, once again, I've added a particularly helpful nugget that highlights the tactics at play within the word choices. May you leverage these to boost your confidence and competence delivering fearless feedback.

INSTANCE FEEDBACK WITH REACTION

The following two examples provide a glimpse into how the conversation can flow, when reactions are most prone to pop up in a conversation, and how to integrate HEAR into HOA. Remember, the reaction you're observing is the external display of the experience. How they are feeling can be very different.

INSTANCE WITH REACTION EXAMPLE 1

This first example demonstrates a performance management situation with an additional behavioral challenge.

A manager in my feedback training course was facing a challenge of someone who missed their call metrics. They recently raised the outbound call expectation from 350 to 500 calls.

The messaging had come from the leadership team, and every other agent responded to the change by increasing their call volume, except for this person.

At play in this scenario were also some assumptions around the person's change adaptability (or lack thereof), and we decided the right entry point for the conversation was the missed metrics to then open the door for a broader conversation about embracing the change.

Manager: Headline

Hey there! I'm hoping you and I can connect today on the topic of metrics. I'm invested in you hitting your numbers and want to get ahead of any hurdles. Do you have some time now?

Manager: Observation

I pulled up metrics for the team and noticed you didn't hit the updated target of 500, and because I've always known you to be dedicated to your performance, I wanted to take some time to talk about moving you from the old target of 350 up to successfully hitting 500.

Manager: Ask

I'd love to open it up to you. What's on your mind for hitting the new target this week?

Them: reacting with explanation and a tone of defeat

Well, yeah, I know the call expectation went up, and I think for other territories, there's enough leads to sustain that volume. My territory is smaller, so it's feeling impossible.

Manager: Hear

Let's pause for a moment. I'm not sure what I'm hearing in your voice: is it frustration? Defeat?

Manager: Explore

Tell me more of what's running through your mind.

Them: [Tone of resignation]

Well, if I'm being honest, it feels short sighted and like it wasn't thought through for what it would mean for each rep. I guess I just feel like I've gotten the short-end of the stick.

Manager: Acknowledge

I can appreciate your perspective and experience processing through this change. Changes in production numbers are rarely easy to digest overnight, and I'm empathetic to what this means for how you manage your pipeline.

Manager: Refocus

While reservations are always fair, what's also true is we still have goals that this team needs to deliver on. We have an opportunity at hand to ensure you're set up for success. What elements of your workflow or pipeline do we want to look at first to help you start getting to 500 calls?

Them

Can we look at the size of my territory and leads and figure out if 500 is even feasible?

[Return back to coach-mode with the Ask step from our HOA feedback delivery framework.]

Manager: Ask

Yes, we certainly can. I can also confidently say, after doing this exercise with a few others, the volume is there.

Yes, we can start there, and then I want to get curious with you. What adjustments within your flow do you want to start thinking about that would help make a difference in your call output?

[Listen and encourage idea generation and self-reflection, and then continue coaching in a forward-looking, solutions-focused manner.]

> *Great, I'm appreciative of your willingness to step up and own your metrics more. Sounds like you're going to take steps x, y, and z.*
> *What feels right for support from me?*

In these situations, the Mindset I find to be empowering is, *"Clear is kind, and unclear is unkind."* Brené Brown shared this with us in her *Dare to Lead* book, and it's so fitting for so many feedback conversations.

Directly, and with care, naming the missed expectation, while communicating in a tone that conveys your curiosity and good intent, contributes to moderating the reaction you'll receive.

Additionally, your ability to manage performance is predicated on ensuring expectations are mutually understood, there is follow up, and support is intentional. Said differently:

**Expectations + Accountability + Support =
Performance Management**

The call expectation here was understood, and by following up to discuss missing the metrics (that's accountability), you're now able to manage performance. Then by helping them to craft their action plan moving forward, you're creating new mutually understood expectations, opening the door for future follow-up, and identifying deliberate support.

Now you're set up for a greater opportunity to influence their performance.

INSTANCE WITH REACTION EXAMPLE 2

If you've ever struggled with what to do when someone shares a personal life insight, this one is for you.

On my team, I had a Weekly Priorities doc. It was a way for us to all get clear and communicate our monthly goals, broken down by weekly priorities.

Each week, folks added their three to five priorities. Then on Friday, everyone updated the status and input the priorities for the following week.

I had a team member who I noticed indicated a couple of priorities were going to be moving over from one week to the next, and I noticed their stress was higher than usual.

I had a choice: address it now, or wait until it was a pattern.

Knowing sooner is always better than later, I stepped into a Mindset that they deserved the benefit of the doubt as this was not typical of their work.

Good thing I did. What ended up happening was a perfect illustration of personal life impacting professional performance. I'm guessing this will resonate deeply.

Manager: Headline

Hey friend! Do you have ten minutes to connect today? My spidey sense tells me we have an opportunity to set you up for more success, and I want to explore priority management with you.

Manager: Observation

I noticed a few of your priorities are spilling over into another week, and because it caught me a bit by surprise, I wanted to see what might be taking up time or mindshare and impacting your deliverables.

Them: [In an exasperated tone, they react with frustration and reasoning.]

Well yeah, this thing is driving me nuts. Honestly, I'm so frustrated. I've been waiting on CX to make a decision on the format, and they're dragging their heels. First they said they'd get back to me last Monday, then they said Thursday. Now we're well past that, and it kinda sucks that it looks bad on me because now I'm missing my deadlines.

Manager: Hear

Alrighty, I'm hearing loud and clear the frustration you're feeling. First and foremost, thank you for your honesty.

Manager: Explore

Okay, so talk to me more about these hurdles and how they're throwing you off your game.

Them: [Their shoulders relax, and their tone shifts.]

So yeah, it's like I make progress, and then they drag their heels. Honestly, I'm just so exhausted that I don't have the energy to keep pursuing.

[They hadn't previously indicated anything in work or life was creating exhaustion although I'd noticed increased stress levels. They've opened a door to what's really going on, so it was time to nudge it open.]

Manager: Explore

Tell me more about this exhaustion.

Them: [On the verge of tears, they open up.]

I haven't told you, but my friend has been diagnosed with cancer. I've been helping out with her kids, and of course I'm happy to help. It's taking a toll as I process what's happening and try to be strong for her and her family. I guess I didn't quite realize how much it was impacting me.

Manager: Acknowledge

Oh my, I'm so, so terribly sorry to hear, and thank you for letting me know what's going on. If I could give you a hug through the computer screen, I absolutely would. It's understandable that the combination of personal exhaustion and being distracted with your friend not only shifts your perspective about what's important and also leaves you with an empty gas tank.

Manager: Refocus

It sounds like we have two areas to tackle: reducing exhaustion and finding the appropriate balance for work. Does that feel right?

Them

Yeah, but honestly I'm not sure what to do. I feel like I'm hanging on by a thread.

Ask

Okay, let's do this. First, it's 2:00, so I want you to sign off. Go take a nap, watch terrible television, or go for a walk—something that will let you take a few deep breaths. You can put on your out of office that people can contact me for anything time sensitive.

Next, let's plan for you and I to reconnect tomorrow and work on a game plan that meets your needs while honoring the priorities for the business.

We have a number of options on the table, and we'll find a path forward.

Does that sound like the right next steps?

In this case, as new information came to light, two of my guiding principles for Mindset began to shine through: care deeply and hold a high bar.

Because I cared deeply for their wellbeing, I put their mental health as the priority, put work on the backburner for an afternoon, and insisted that they disconnect and take a breather.

They were able to come back the next day being mildly refreshed, feeling a weight had been lifted off their shoulders because they weren't hiding what was impacting them.

Now imagine if I hadn't used HEAR.

Imagine I'd blown right through the "speed bump" and hadn't gotten curious about the exhaustion. Instead of a weight lifted, they would've felt the boulder on their back being more restrictive because not only were they emotionally drained, now they would've been feeling the pressure of knowing their manager was seeing their misses.

Then there's how I held a high bar. There was a choice in that moment: let them off the hook with deep empathy, or be their partner through a tough situation.

I've been around the block enough times to know that when things are hard outside of work, many folks seek relief and distraction at work.

By saying we'll revisit and gameplan the following day, I'm still holding an appropriately high bar.

In this case, we did come up with a game plan: I was able to help unblock some of the hurdles, and get them back on track.

Do you want to take a guess as to what happened with our Relationship?

It got stronger. They felt more comfortable letting me know how both they, and their friend, were doing. Win-win-win.

If you're curious about what to do if the outside distraction is even more significant, don't worry, I'll be diving more into when personal impacts professional in Chapter 12.

PATTERN FEEDBACK WITH REACTION

Not surprisingly, Pattern conversations can spark reactions. Remember the analogy of feedback being like having food in your teeth. The more food that's stuck in your teeth, the more you might feel frustrated, annoyed, or embarrassed that it's there.

Let's look at two tricky and emotional situations. As you read through, don't forget to underline the words and phrases that strike you most. I share all of this language with the goal that you'll feel empowered to say what needs to be said and to make the language your own.

PATTERN WITH REACTION EXAMPLE 3

If you've ever had an employee completely shut down, this one is for you. If you've ever had someone turn around and blame you, this is also up your alley.

I bring this situation to you by way of a brilliant leader who sought out my help in turning around this baffling interaction.

What you're about to read is what was initially shared as feedback, followed by my guidance on how to handle the reaction differently next time. All of the employee responses after her camera turning off are assumed responses based on previous experience with this person.

Manager: Headline

Before we wrap up our one-to-one meeting, I'd like to offer coaching on cross-functional communication, all through the lens of helping you get to your next level. Mind if I share?

Manager: Observation

I've noticed a change in both your type and volume of communication, not just with me but also with finance and sales. Formerly, your DMs and emails had a proactive nature to them and a tone of collaboration.

Now your notes are coming off as more demanding and are missing the problem-solving nature you'd formerly been communicating with.

[Team member turns off her camera on Zoom.]

Manager: Hear

Oh, let me pause here, I'm seeing you just turned your camera off.

Manager: Explore

Talk to me about what's running through your mind.

Them

Yeah, I heard what you said, and I gotta go.

[Team member hangs up the Zoom call.]

Before I share what to do next, let me call out that there's great risk in a situation like this. You may get pulled out of Fearless Feedback and no longer operate at the intersection of Mindset, Relationship, and Delivery.

It is absolutely fair that these behaviors (silence, turning off the camera, and hanging up) activate reactions with you. You're human. And what's also true is there's only one person who gets to be emotional in this, and it's not you, not now.

Next, turning off a camera and hanging up a call are two signs of distress, and the Relationship is at risk. What I'm going to share next is to be communicated with a fair, caring, yet firm and clear tone and delivery.

Manager: [Text/DM them immediately.]

Hey there! I'm concerned you signed off in the middle of our conversation. Please sign back in, so we can finish chatting.

Them: [No Response and no dialing back in.]

Manager: [Call them and get their voicemail.]

Hey there! I'm calling to express concern that you've ignored my text requesting you to dial back in. Please call me back asap as this is not how you and I are going to engage. I respect our relationship, and you, too much.

Them: [They call back.]

Hey, I got your message.

Manager: Transition

Thank you for responding to my voicemail.

It is always absolutely fair to have a reaction to any feedback and coaching I share with you. What there isn't space for in our dynamic is disrespect. I'm far too invested in you and your wellbeing, and hanging up, giving up on our work together, is not something that should happen again.

[Dive back into HEAR, picking up where you left off.]

Manager: Explore

Help me understand what drove your impulse to shut down your camera and leave the call.

Them

It felt like I was being attacked, and honestly I had a moment of panic. But also it was feeling one sided. You said my communication has changed; well so has yours.

[Resist the urge to defend yourself; get curious and stay the course.]

Manager: Explore

Tell me more of what you're meaning about my communication.

Them

You haven't been helping me to draft comms or sending your preview notes to partners, and my plate has been too full to pick up those extra bits.

Manager: Acknowledge

First, thank you for your honesty. Speaking openly, and with respect, is how we'll get through this blip on the radar. I can also appreciate your perspective about my role in your work.

Manager: Refocus

And while it's true I've backed off of those pieces, I can appreciate that I was not transparent enough in communicating why I was backing off, so I will own that piece. What's also true is those comms are part of your role and part of you leading these events. Would that be a fair characterization of the challenge we need to address and solve today?

[With the emotion and core issue identified, it's time to step fully into coach-mode to move towards greater clarity, alignment, and action.]

Manager: Ask

Great, so let's reframe the topic of today's conversation. Rather than cross-functional communication, let's revisit communication ownership.

Are you willing to explore with me the various points of communication that will set you up for success and what's to be owned by each of us moving forward?

There are a number of things to call out here.

Your people might not dramatically hang up on you, but silence as a reaction is just as powerful and important to be addressed.

Secondly, being caring and direct with our messaging is not a permission slip to walk all over us. You are not a doormat. When someone exhibits disrespectful behavior, you can and should notice the boundary crossing, notice the relationship is now at risk, and seek to correct and repair quickly.

Finally, sometimes reactions can help us surface core issues. It can be fair that you pivot the topic of feedback, which was modeled at the end here. This type of pivot can strengthen clarity and ultimately improve trust within your relationship.

PATTERN WITH REACTION EXAMPLE 4

This next situation was a person on my team, a subject matter expert whose institutional knowledge was incredibly valuable. This person had a tendency to blame others, not take accountability, and on a few big projects, miss deadlines.

On top of that, they only ever did exactly what was asked of them, leaving stakeholders a bit frustrated to find themselves in a back and forth with this person.

Going back to our tactic of Name It to Tame It, I had a few paths I could have pursued with this conversation: stakeholder management, deadlines, and strategic thinking.

What I decided to name this when I addressed it was "ownership," because, at the end of the day, seeing a 10% lift in ownership would have positively impacted all the other areas.

Admittedly, this situation was incredibly frustrating to me. My first challenge was parsing through my own narrative of the situation to dial into the true behavior needing to be addressed.

As you read through, underline the phrasing that stands out to you. And if you've worked with me in real life, I'm guessing you're very much going to hear my voice as you read this.

Manager: Headline

I want to connect with you on an opportunity to take your work to the next level, and it's on the topic of ownership. Do you have time to explore with me now?

Manager: Observation

Great, so as I just mentioned, the topic is ownership. I'm noticing a pattern with your larger projects, most specifically this last training video project where I didn't see you take the level of ownership I'd expect for your level and experience.

What I observed at each milestone check-in was an explanation that pointed to faulting others. What I didn't see was you truly owning this project.

Because I care about you continuing to grow and elevate in your career, I wouldn't be doing right by you if I didn't highlight this as a growth area and a differentiator for you moving forward.

[On the video call, I see them shifting in their seat, almost biting their tongue to hold back.]

Manager: Hear

I'm noticing you're wanting to jump in.

Manager: Explore

Go for it . . . tell me what's running through your mind.

Them

Well, yes, for this training video, I've had to wait on ops, and then I was waiting for a signoff from their leader. At every step, there was a hurdle beyond my control.

Manager: Acknowledge

You're not wrong. Hurdles do come up, and it's the very nature of our role as the connective tissue that we need to navigate these complexities.

Manager: Refocus

What's also true is for you to reach your next level, to reach the level of influence you're wanting to have in this org, you have an opportunity to take ownership of each of these hurdles. Taking, for example, the reasoning you just shared about ops and their leader, pretend for a moment that you stood in a place of ownership of the scenario. What's one thing you might have done differently?

[I can see their frustration is on the rise, and they're trying to keep it under wraps. It's simultaneously feeling a bit like the mindblown emoji, as if they're wrapping their head around considering if and how things could have been different.]

Them

To be honest, I don't think I could have done anything differently.

[This is now a coaching opportunity because some sense of being defeated has creeped into their tone. I shift back into the Ask step of the feedback framework.]

Manager: Ask

What I'm about to do is challenge you, and because I believe you're capable of great things, please accept this challenge for what it is: a coaching opportunity to make you even more impactful within this team.

Pretend for a moment you had a magic wand and you went back in time. Ops is dragging their feet, yet you're accountable for the outcomes on your project. Through that lens, what comes to mind?

Them

I guess what I could've done was get time on the calendar and do a walkthrough, and maybe ask them what barriers they anticipated, so I wouldn't know about it after the fact.

Manager

Boom! There you go. What else?

Them

I guess asking them what else they need from me for them to hit their deliverables?

Manager: Ask

Now you're onto it. That's the difference between taking ownership or passively directing a project.

And while we've been using this most recent project as the case study, this is a pattern I'm seeing when I reflect on your last few deliverables.

Here's what I'd like to ask of you, now having a stronger idea of what I'm meaning by ownership: what's a commitment you want to make to yourself for taking more ownership on your next project?

[Listen, encourage solutions and actions, and focus on alignment and support to wrap up the conversation.]

What did you notice you underlined in reading this exchange?

Did you notice the coaching pivot? If we're serious about feedback being for someone's development, then we need to be serious about being their coach and development partner.

Did you notice how I brought back the pattern callout at the end? This conversation was not about this one project; it was about a pattern of behavior, with the most recent example being the vehicle in which to discuss the pattern.

ROLE FIT WITH REACTION

ROLE FIT WITH REACTION EXAMPLE 5

This last scenario is one in which I surprised myself, and in an important way it ended up helping me make a decision about someone who I was questioning was a fit for the role.

I was onboarding a new hire. From the get-go, I had doubts. The person who showed up for training was not the same person we interviewed.

During training, which was a small onboarding class of just three folks, his quantity of Stussy "S" symbols drawn dramatically outpaced his volume of notes taken. Yes, Stussy symbols, the popular 90s apparel brand.

As we transitioned from training in the conference room to getting on the phones with clients, more red flags began to present themselves. He was overly casual, bordering on unprofessional, with everyone: peers, advertisers, and even our head of sales.

On calls, he didn't follow call frameworks, segments of which required legal compliance.

Multiple feedback conversations, addressing multiple concerning patterns, had already happened. My Mindset was one of frustration moving toward resolution. I knew things were coming to a head, and I was needing to push a bit to get to a decision point about his fit in the role.

From a Relationship standpoint, I owed it to him to be as frank as possible, so he was clear that his fate was in his hands.

It's worth highlighting that what you're about to read is not common. In more than twenty years of a management career, I've taken this approach only three times.

Manager: Headline

Thank you for joining me for a quick conversation. There's a decent probability that what I'm about to say is going to be uncomfortable. I also wouldn't be doing right by you if I didn't candidly say I have concerns about your ability to be successful in this role.

[He stood quietly as I went on.]

Manager: Observation

Between the frequency of conversations we've been having and the lack of immediate change and implementation, my concerns about you being a fit for this role are growing.

Manager: Ask

*Heading into this three-day weekend, I'd like to ask that you spend time thinking about the extent to which you give a sh*t about this job.*

[His eyes went big, presumably because he wasn't anticipating this level of directness.]

Them

YES! Of course I care about the job. Why would you even question it?

Manager: Hear

I'm seeing you're surprised, and to be honest, that concerns me.

Manager: Explore

After the feedback conversations we've had in the last four weeks about professionalism, language accuracy, and attention to detail, help me understand the surprise you're conveying right now.

Them

Well yeah, we talked about those things, but that doesn't mean I don't care about doing well here.

Manager: Acknowledge

Okay, I can appreciate your perspective. You're not seeing a connection between disregarding feedback and care for the role.

Manager: Refocus

What's incredibly important within this role and this team is aligning actions and behaviors.

Manager: Ask

Now that I've jolted you a bit, and you're seeing the seriousness of taking action on the feedback you've already received over the last four weeks, I'd like to ask that you spend the weekend reflecting on how you can demonstrate your engagement and commitment to this role by being a team member who takes seriously the feedback and coaching you're receiving.

Will you do that this weekend?

Them

Yeah, I'll try, but I do have a wedding I'm going to.

I kid you not, that's literally how he responded.

I share this example for a few reasons.

First, as they say, desperate times can call for desperate measures. When your intuition tells you that you're not getting through to someone, listen to your gut.

That's what I did here. My instinct told me I needed to get dramatic to capture his attention because nothing else seemed to be sinking in.

Secondly, I believe in having the right tools in your toolbelt. Not every tool is meant for every situation, and taking care with your tool selection matters. As I noted, the method used in this conversation is one I use sparingly but appropriately.

Finally, even in these challenging moments, we can still operate within the Fearless Feedback Framework. I want to call out a few particular phrases that are great examples of strong Delivery as a result of an intentional Mindset and staying in Relationship with them:

- There's a decent probability that what I'm about to say is going to be uncomfortable.

- I also wouldn't be doing right by you if I didn't candidly say . . .

- Help me understand the surprise you're conveying right now.

- I can appreciate your perspective . . .

To save the suspense, about two weeks later, we parted ways with him. In that conversation, when I used my standard termination line (*"We've made the difficult decision to part ways with you, and today is going to be your last day."*), his honest response in front of our HR person was, *"But why?"*

CHAPTER SUMMARY

This chapter is arguably the heart of this book, modeling real situations that are initially difficult. As these examples illustrate, conversations get easier, and tension can be released when we're at the empowering intersection of Mindset, Relationship, and Delivery.

With each conversation and each reaction, we can root ourselves in a strong inner game, ensuring trust and safety while in conversation and being clear and intentional with our word choices.

I invite you to pause and take note of what is shifting in how you're thinking and feeling about delivering feedback and handling reactions. Feel free to reach out directly to me. I'd love to hear from you: katie@enduranceboss.com.

Using the Fearless Feedback Framework

FOLLOWING UP AFTER FEEDBACK

You've had the conversation. You clearly, and with care, gave direct feedback that then pivoted into a coaching interaction where you two were able to co-create ideas for action. You navigated their reaction, and you're now thinking, *"What's next?"*

I'd like to suggest three avenues for following up on a feedback conversation.

These should not be viewed as a checklist or requirements after each conversation. Rather, these three actions can help increase implementation of feedback while ensuring you're investing in your relationship.

DOCUMENTATION

When I joined my last organization, I had no fewer than three managers tell me a version of this message: *"HR won't let me fire anyone."*

I found this odd for two reasons:

1. I'd only ever been in company cultures that moved swiftly in cases of poor performance.

2. I was a member of the people team, so I knew this was not fully accurate.

The key is appropriate documentation, and it must follow when you've had meaningful conversations about performance, behavior, or impact.

Let me start with what documentation is not:

- A brutal rehashing of their shortfalls

- A note in someone's personnel file

- A threatening message

- A burn book

Documentation enables us to ensure we have a clear, mutual understanding of next steps. Good documentation also creates an opportunity to convey support and belief in our people's ability to pivot and make progress.

My documentation has typically taken the form of an email for three core reasons.

- First, in the case that performance doesn't turn around, or someone continues with behaviors that put them on a path to being a Role Fit concern, I need a time-stamped paper trail.

- Secondly, if I'm only documenting behaviors, conversations, and reactions in a doc, that creates a one-sided view of the situation, which means the notes might be contested.

•   Finally, I want to capture their reaction and response within the paper trail.

My greatest hope when I send a post-feedback conversation recap email is that I never need it as evidence that would impact their standing in their role. But in the case it goes in the direction of needing to separate with the person, these emails help to expedite the process with HR.

Because this book is rooted in helping you to know *how* to take these actions, here are a few samples of post-feedback email documentation.

EXAMPLE 1

Hey ___!

Thank you for making time to chat today.

I know it wasn't an easy conversation, and I'm appreciative of the disappointment you were feeling.

I also know I wouldn't be doing right by you if I didn't bring to light this blind spot in your communication.

As a recap of the action steps we discussed, here's how you're planning to take your communication to the next level:

*   • XX*

*   • XX*

*   • XX*

What else would you like to add or adjust?

I believe in you and am here to support you.

EXAMPLE 2

Hi ____,

Thank you for joining me today.

For the sake of transparency and enabling our alignment, I've captured what we discussed today.

You absolutely have amazing strengths, and I believe this will just be a blip on the radar on your path to ongoing growth and development.

To get back on track, we're going to focus on your inputs: open calls, pipeline management, and appointment rates. Improving these three will yield stronger outputs.

Anything else you want to prioritize after thinking more about our chat?

You can do it, and I'm committed to empowering your journey!

EXAMPLE 3

This next example was one I sent after we'd had three to four interactions (live conversations and exchanges in direct messages), and they continued to miss their timelines, providing explanations rather than taking ownership. My concerns about their ability to be successful in the role were growing.

I share this example because our intent with these emails is not to scare our people; our goal is alignment and progress. In situations when nothing is changing and things are still slipping through the cracks, a more direct email can be needed.

In the end, this email did end up getting used as a proof point to move them out of the role.

Hey Brian!

I'm reaching back out as accountability is a big piece of success and execution.

Have you been able to wrap up the needs analysis? The initial commitment was 1/15, then Monday, then Thursday, and I want to be sure you're able to move the ball forward, so our employee onboarding isn't impacted.

I'd appreciate seeing what you have so far and supporting you in every way possible.

Thanks,

Katie

It's worth calling out that not every feedback or coaching conversation requires an email follow-up.

If you're operating in the High Cadence, Low Stakes mentality of feedback (which I hope you will adopt), sending a ping or note after every single nugget of coaching would likely be overkill.

Here are the instances when I send a written recap, for which the level of urgency will depend on the situation:

- **Performance pattern**: They didn't take action or get enough traction when I addressed performance initially, and adding a dose of urgency to the conversation by following up in writing can help move the needle more quickly.

- **Spidey sense**: This is not scientific, and I also believe managers should listen to their intuition. If your gut is telling you they might not work out in the role, and an objective fly on the wall would assess the situation similarly, do yourself a favor and send the supportive recap note. Best case, you never need it. Worst case, you're prepared and can partner more effectively with HR to initiate changes.

- **Unacceptable behavior**: There have been instances where someone acted too abruptly or inappropriately that a serious message of *"This can never happen again"* is warranted. These are few and far between, and in your entire management career, you'll hopefully only observe a few.

In these more serious situations, I've also used my recap email to manage up to my leader and to my HR business partner.

After I send it directly to my team member, depending on the situation and how they handled the conversation, I might forward it to my leader to give them a heads-up on the performance challenge at hand. In that note, I'll indicate that I'm sharing for the sake of keeping them in the loop. I'll also give an early indication on how and where I think the situation will land. More on how to decide when it's time to let someone go in Chapter 11.

When it comes to positive feedback, sending a glowing follow-up email can be extremely beneficial as well.

- First, it can serve as a positive paper trail that might serve you both when the time comes to discuss a promotion or role expansion.

- Secondly, don't underestimate how often people receive fantastic notes of appreciation and forward it along to loved ones.

CHECKING IN

Our second consideration for post-feedback follow-up is a simple check-in conversation.

The phrasing is less important than the intention and sentiment. On a human level, how are they feeling after the feedback conversation? That's what we're getting at.

Below are samples of how this might sound:

- How are you doing since we connected for our last conversation?

- What else has come to mind that you'd value chatting through?

- How'd our conversation land for you?

Ask the question, and then hold space for their response.

Each of us has a fundamental need to feel seen and heard. This is your opportunity to see and hear them. They've had time to digest the conversation and your coaching, and thoughts and feelings likely have surfaced.

Checking back in sends a message that you care, and open and honest conversations are always on the table within your working relationship.

CLEARING THE AIR

Not all conversations go as planned. We're human, and we can react or communicate in a way that we don't intend.

For that reason, a third post-feedback conversation consideration is to clear the air. Our Fearless Feedback Framework can help us succeed in these moments as well.

MINDSET: PROCESS YOUR EMOTIONS

To effectively clear the air, we've got to get our head right first.

You will not have a productive conversation if your emotions are still in charge.

Whatever anger, frustration, or annoyance you're feeling, find a healthy way to process. Is that a walk around the block? Jumping onto a hard Peloton class? Journaling? Singing Alanis Morissette at the top of your lungs?

You do you, and then ask yourself these questions:

- What's important to me about repairing this situation?

- What happens if there's no repair?

When we make it matter, we make it happen.

RELATIONSHIP: CLARIFY YOUR INTENTION

Your next step is thinking about your Relationship by having clarity on what you Do and Don't want to happen in this follow up conversation.

The authors of Crucial Conversations[6], call this a Contrasting Statement: *"a tool to create safety and clarify intent when a conversation goes off track or someone misinterprets your motives."*

For example, a chat over a video call went off the rails, and you're feeling deeply disrespected.

You Don't want to point fingers. You Do want to understand the tension.

You Don't want to make assumptions. You Do want to restore your partnership.

Know what you Do and Don't want to see happen, and you'll be better prepared to achieve your goal.

RELATIONSHIP: OWN YOUR PART

The feedback conversation went sideways. They reacted by blaming you for not being clear enough with expectations. You then felt (and acted) a bit defensive as you can't imagine how you could have been more clear.

You could cut the tension with a knife. You both walked away from the situation feeling frustrated.

For the sake of repair, what are you willing to own within the situation?

Were you short on time and so more curt than normal? Did you operate under the assumption that you'd been clear, and there's room to explore what might not have been mutually understood?

It's not an easy question to ask, and the best managers,

6 Kerry Patterson, et al *Crucial Conversations*, 2012, pg 84-85

leaders, and communicators challenge themselves to reflect: *what can I own in the role I played in this situation?*

This isn't about taking responsibility for their actions.

It's about acknowledging that it takes two parties to create a relationship, and you need a path forward to communicating together productively.

DELIVERY: NAME IT TO TAME IT

Next up, we revisit our handy tactic, Name It to Tame It.

This is about naming the elephant in the room. Whether you're in person and can approach them at the water cooler, or you're needing to DM/email when they're remote, either way, Name It to Tame It.

Your opening can sound like this:

> *Yesterday's conversation didn't go how either you or I would have hoped, and I value you too much to let the tension linger. Would you be open to revisiting? My hope would be to clear the air, so we both feel seen and heard and can get things back on track.*

Then look for time on their calendar.

If in person, I highly recommend getting a coffee and walking around the block. Then you're shoulder to shoulder instead of across a conference room table, which can feel more confrontational.

DELIVERY: OPEN THE CONVERSATION

You've set up time to chat. Maybe you're going for a walk, or you're dialing into a call.

Now you get to put all the pieces together to stay grounded and then shift into problem-solving mode with them:

1. Mindset: Process your emotions.

2. Relationship: Clarify your intention.

3. Relationship: Own your part.

4. Delivery: Name it to tame it.

Here's how I've tended to flow in these instances:

As I mentioned in my note, that conversation didn't go how you or I would have hoped.

I'd like to revisit as I don't want us to have tension, and I do want to clear the way for continuing to work well together.

We have the same goals, and my sense is we can revisit how we're approaching.

From my perspective, something I'd like to own that I failed to do _____ well, and for that I apologize.

[They typically accept the apology and offer their own.]

Great, so we've identified something we each can commit to doing differently should we find ourselves in this spot again.

What else feels important for us to revisit or get out in the open?

What are other important ways we can strengthen how we communicate when our frustrations get the better of us?

[You're now in a place of honesty and feeling seen and heard, which is good!]

Now, wrap up with a specific show of gratitude and recap the commitment you're making to them as a result of this clearing the air conversation. Something like:

* I'm appreciative of your willingness to revisit yesterday's conversation. I'm committed to looping back to you more frequently to ensure there's no grey area in your goals.

* Thank you for your openness and the honesty you shared today. I'm invested in our working relationship and commit to asking better questions to ensure understanding.

WHEN THINGS ARE BEYOND REPAIR

Repair takes courage. Even if the outcome isn't perfect, your willingness to step into the hard conversation is what sets you apart as a leader.

This approach for Clearing the Air works with folks who report to you, peers, cross-functional partners, and even those above you on the org chart.

As a manager, I've yet to have a scenario where the dynamics with someone on my team was beyond repair. I'll even go so far as to say that great managers don't get the luxury of writing off someone who reports to them.

What's also true is that other relationships around the business can be different. There can be a cross-functional person with whom you struggle to see eye to eye, and your clearing the air effort wasn't well received.

There's one question I encourage you to ask: *am I proud of how I've shown up?*

If yes, let that keep you grounded. You cannot control the behavior of others; you can ensure you're proud of your behavior.

You might need to let it roll off your back. It might be that you need to remove yourself from the situation. Make the decision that is right for you.

CHAPTER SUMMARY

Your job is not done once you've had the feedback conversation. There are three actions that can make sense, depending on the situation.

1. **Document**: Send an email recap that is clear and supportive. The intention is increasing alignment and clarity for the growth opportunity and next steps.

2. **Check in**: Loop back and see how they're doing. It's a simple way to send a message of care while offering an opportunity for any follow-up conversation.

3. **Clear the air**: If the situation got the better of you, repair is important. You can do that by maintaining a strong mindset, clarifying your intention, owning your part, naming that things are off, and opening up an honest conversation.

ADDRESSING WHEN FEEDBACK HASN'T BEEN IMPLEMENTED

After a good conversation, they appeared to be game to invest in this area of development, but you aren't seeing implementation. Your brain is having a bit of a *"wtf"* reaction, and you begin to wonder what you did "wrong."

First it's important to recognize why folks might not implement feedback from their manager. There are three primary reasons:

- Actionability

- Buy-in

- Accountability

ACTIONABILITY: THE *HOW*

I see this regularly with my coaching clients. They receive feedback from their leader, and they're unsure *how* to take action. Because they don't know how, they feel stumped, and they're perceived as not actioning on feedback they've been given.

For example, one lovely human I was working with was told in her performance review that she needed to *"be more strategic."*

She came to me and asked if I could help her.

My first question was, *"What does 'being more strategic' look and feel like?"*

She wasn't sure. Her leader had just said that this is where she needs to be stronger if she wanted a promotion.

Was her leader wanting to see more proactive communication? Or was it how far into the future she was planning? Maybe there's something about connecting inputs to outputs? She sure didn't know.

Without a sense for what improvement looks like, it's awfully hard to know how to improve.

If you're seeing someone not taking action, your first gut check is to get curious about the extent to which your feedback interaction truly pivoted into a coaching conversation. Remember my rule of thumb: feedback without action is simply criticism.

Using this example of *"being more strategic,"* imagine how differently she would have felt if her manager had leaned into these coaching questions:

- Let's start by aligning on what strategic thinking is. You go first: what comes to mind when you hear that term? [Listen then build further.] Here's what it means to me . . .

- Imagine six months from now you're more confidently and competently modeling being a strategic team member. What do you imagine might be some key ingredients in getting there?

- What initial ideas come to mind for what will help you to grow within this area?

- What support would you like from me on this journey to strengthening your strategic work?

If you're not seeing traction, start by reflecting on how you coached them to identify meaningful actions for improvement.

BUY-IN: THE *WHY*

I'm guilty of this one.

I once received feedback that I need to tone down my energy when leading group trainings.

I've consciously not implemented this feedback. I've continued to play music and bring my A game to every single training session.

The reason?

My energy is my superpower. In fact, in the last year before writing this book, three large organizations stated that my energy and how I engage an audience were the *main* reasons they decided to work with me to train their managers.

When I think about receiving feedback to back off and be less engaging, I'm still unclear *why* it would be to my benefit to do so.

If your people aren't feeling the feedback is in their self-interest or aligned with where they want to take their career, they're less likely to take action.

Let me recommend a two-fold solution here:

1. Reevaluate the feedback.

2. Revisit your Headline.

REEVALUATE THE FEEDBACK

Contrary to popular belief, not *all* feedback is a gift.

Gifts are things given to us with care and with our interests, well-being, and aspirations in mind.

Not all feedback fits that bill.

You tell me: do both of these feel like gifts you'd value?

- A random candle, still in a plastic shopping bag, left on your desk with your name on a post-it

- Your favorite artist's latest album, beautifully wrapped, delivered to you with a handwritten card

All gifts were not created equal, and neither is feedback.

If there's a chance your team member is not bought into the feedback, you need to reevaluate whether this is valuable feedback.

Is this one-off feedback or a pattern? To what extent does this feedback connect with their overall goals?

If the feedback is going to serve them, their interests, and their overall ability to be successful in their role (and future career), then yes, you did the right thing by sharing.

If after further consideration, you realize your feedback might have been received as a random candle in a plastic bag (versus the thoughtful record you knew they'd love), then yes, their probability for implementation will naturally be low.

REVISIT YOUR HEADLINE

If your team member hasn't bought into the *why* of your feedback, and the feedback is truly aligned with their self-interests and goals, then you likely need to revisit your conversation opener: your Headline.

How you lead into the conversation sets the tone for how the message will be received.

Below are two quick examples:

- I'm wanting to connect on an area I believe will serve you as you continue growing in your role. Do you have a few minutes to connect on executive presence?

- I'm seeing a way for you to have a greater impact within the team, and it's related to flexibility. Could we connect this afternoon and chat through?

These Headlines have three features:

1. Sending a message of good intent

2. Focusing on their self-interest

3. Asking permission

You'll increase buy-in and therefore feedback implementation by leveraging their self-interest.

ACCOUNTABILITY: THE FOLLOW-THROUGH

Without a plan and accountability, action slips.

It's one of the reasons 43% of people throw in the towel

on their New Year's resolution before the month of January is even over.[7]

In fact, "studies show that people who not only write their goals but set up a way to be accountable for them will be 2x as likely to achieve them."[8]

There's great news for you: you can build accountability planning into your feedback conversations!

In practice, here is how it can sound:

Headline

Do you have a few minutes to connect? I'm noticing a potential blind spot that I don't want to get in your way as you continue developing in your role.

Observation

I'm noticing a tendency for you to take on a condescending tone when you're talking with Sarah. Because it's rather unlike how I see you engage with everyone else within the accounting team, I wouldn't be doing right by you if I didn't bring it to you today.

[They appear both frustrated and relieved. You help them feel seen and heard via the HEAR framework. Then you jump back to the Ask.]

Ask

Here's what I'd propose: let's take a few minutes to openly and honestly get curious about what activates this tone when you're working with Sarah. My sense is if we can surface the point of activation, we can more effectively

7 Richard Batts, "Why Most New Year's Resolutions Fail," Lead Read Today, The Ohio State University, February 2, 2023, https://fisher.osu.edu/blogs/leadreadtoday/why-most-new-years-resolutions-fail

8 ibid

identify actions you want to take to keep it from getting the better of you.

[They share what drives them wild and causes them to change how they're communicating, and they identify actions they want to take to keep their reaction in check.]

[Now create accountability.]

What feels right for you and I to follow up on as you're trying these actions?

What role would you like me to play in supporting your efforts, especially when we're in meetings with Sarah?

Most likely, they'll ask for reminders or progress checks. Then add them to your standing one-to-one meeting agenda, so you're able to easily revisit the feedback and support their development efforts.

Without follow up, action will slip.

Build accountability alignment into your initial feedback conversations, and you'll more easily be able to broach the topic of feedback implementation because doing so is following up on what you've already committed to do.

COMMON MANAGER QUESTION

If you're thinking, *"What do I do when they still don't implement feedback,"* I've got you covered!

You've ensured your feedback is actionable, and they've bought into why this feedback serves them. You've followed up, but they still haven't implemented changes.

What do you do?

You address it head on. What follows is how a real conversation might go with a breakdown to highlight the specific word choices that make this language effective.

Manager: Headline

I'd love to connect with you today on something I'm concerned is going to hold you back from being well-positioned for what's next. The topic is feedback implementation. Do you have a few minutes?

Manager: Observation

I can't help but notice that you haven't yet taken action on the feedback we spoke about regarding the process changes we made earlier this year. From our conversation, you gave a green light for understanding and moving forward.

Manager: Ask

I'm interested in better understanding what's gotten in the way and how you're thinking about getting things back on track.

Them: [In a matter-of-fact, nonchalant way they offer an explanation.]

It's just been really busy, and I guess I've defaulted to the old way of doing things just to keep up with everything.

[Sensing a bit of resistance or resignation in their tone, you pause to explore what might be lingering under the surface.]

Manager: Hear

Let's pause for a hot moment. My spidey sense is telling me there might be more to it.

Manager: Explore

Tell me more from your perspective.

Them

It's just that this is our busiest time of year. If I'm being honest, it doesn't feel like the right time to be changing our processes and then coming down on us when we've also got these numbers to hit before the quarter wraps up.

Manager: Acknowledge

You're right; the timing is very much a challenge. You're not wrong there.

Manager: Refocus

What's also true is that not adopting these changes is going to start to set you back next quarter because the old way will no longer be accessible. I don't want you to take a hit in your efficiency or performance.

[Return to Ask from our HOA feedback framework.]

Manager: Ask

What are you seeing as the first step you want to take toward implementing the updated process? And what do you want to commit to as your second step after that?

[They share one to two action steps.]

As you're taking these steps, what feels right in how we reconnect and revisit your progress? What support can I lend as you hit hurdles on your learning curve?

Here's a summary of deliberate word choices and why this approach consistently works:

- You cannot tame what you do not name. We named it: *"The topic is feedback implementation."*

- Clear is kind, and unclear is unkind. You're sharing the observation directly: *"I can't help but notice that you haven't yet taken action . . . "*

- You're focused on the future, not rehashing their explanations.

- You're making two things true at the same time: a lot can be going on *and* changes need to be made.

- You're having them create the actions: *"What are you seeing as the first step you want to take toward implementing the updated process?"*

- You're using *you*, not *we* in action planning, which sends a powerful message of ownership.

- You're setting up accountability follow-up.

- You're offering support.

In my experience, most managers never have this conversation. It feels confrontational. It feels micromanage-y. That is, until you internalize that caring deeply and holding a high bar (two of our Mindset guiding principles) requires us to show up for our people. If they aren't taking action on feedback we thoughtfully delivered—feedback that's in service of their well-being and career growth—the kindest thing to do is to approach it directly (with care and curiosity).

It's possible you might now be thinking, *"What do I do if that still doesn't work?"*

My punchline is this: you can't want it more than they do.

If you're still not getting traction despite the techniques shared in this chapter, consider the extent to which they *want* to remain and progress in their role.

It's feasible you'll then proceed into a Role Fit conversation to explore their desire to retain their role.

CHAPTER SUMMARY

It's easy to feel frustrated when we don't see our folks adopting and implementing the feedback we've carefully shared. To increase the probability of action being taken, remember these:

- **Actionability**: Do they know *how* to take action?

- **Buy-in**: Do they know *why* this is to their benefit?

- **Accountability**: Was there meaningful follow-up?

DECIDING WHEN TO LET SOMEONE GO

One of the hardest decisions a manager has to make is whether to keep or part ways with a team member. With our increasingly remote and global work teams, it's not getting any easier.

This is one of the reasons determining the purpose of the feedback (Instance, Pattern, or Role Fit) is the first step for managers to take before embarking into a Fearless Feedback conversation.

It becomes easier to gain clarity on where someone might stand when you pause to consider whether someone's behaviors (and actions) have moved beyond Pattern into Role Fit concerns.

Because we're human, and humans are complex, let me introduce three additional filters to help in your decision-making:

1. Rate of improvement

2. Operating level

3. Cultural impact

RATE OF IMPROVEMENT

I had a team member who was pure joy. Lifeblood within the team and office. The joke-teller, the one you go to for a smile on a tough day. A straight up solid human.

He was on the struggle bus with his role. Deadlines were often missed, quality of work wasn't to our team's level of excellence, and working autonomously was difficult.

I was coaching and giving feedback along the way. I was having follow-up conversations for accountability when things were missed. Conversations had been documented, and I'd been keeping my leader and HR partner up to date.

He was trying his damnedest, but his rate of growth and improvement was not keeping up with the needs of the business.

If I'd had six months or a year to help him develop, he likely could have been successful. We didn't have that kind of time. The pace of the business was eclipsing his speed of improvement.

The rest of the team was already picking up his slack, and despite him being a wonderful human and joy to be around, after a few months it became increasingly clear that he couldn't keep up with the needs of the business.

As it became clear, I then moved quickly.

He knew he was struggling. The team saw him struggling. Experience has shown me that waiting too long can be detrimental to the person and the team.

No one likes to struggle, yet he showed up every day, gave it his best, and continued to not meet the mark. That doesn't feel good. No one wants to end work every day knowing they're not meeting expectations.

On a team level, your team spots underperformance and personnel issues often before you do. The longer you hold onto someone who everyone else knows isn't pulling their weight, the more damage you'll do to your team's culture.

I decided to let him go.

My decision to part ways was solidified when multiple people informed me the full extent to which they'd been covering for him and carrying his load.

After you've identified that your feedback needs to progress from Pattern to Role Fit, your next mental filter is evaluating their rate of improvement against the pace of business growth.

In making that determination, it can be helpful to ask yourself: *what do I owe them, the team, and the company?*

This question helps surface tension points between your efforts to support the individual compared to the impact on the team and company.

You owe your team member an honest assessment and active management of the situation. Your team deserves fairness and consistency in performance expectations. As the manager, you are responsible for minimizing risk (poor customer experiences, costly errors, etc) for your company.

If the team member can keep up, and progress is steady, you have a good chance of a turnaround situation.

If progress is slow, and the needs of the business are outpacing them, the kindest thing to do might be to make the call to part ways.

OPERATING LEVEL

No less difficult is when we have a more tenured team member, and we begin to see a mismatch in how they're operating compared to their title and level.

I was working with a brilliant leader on this very struggle. She had a team member who had a director title but was operating as a manager.

Directors within this organization are expected to work independently, make strategic decisions on behalf of the business, and truly be a master within their domain.

Based on the observed actions and behaviors, this person needed a lot of support. They requested their leader double-check their work, didn't take the lead to make recommendations for action, and were not able to present to the leadership team without massive prep and coaching.

Their operating level was not aligned with their expected level of performance.

There was a choice to be made: continue extreme support to help them get the job done, or find someone else who can operate at the appropriate level to meet the needs of the organization. A change was made, and now the entire team is operating more smoothly with everyone meeting or exceeding the expectations of their level.

Clear criteria is what enabled this leader to make the call to part ways with this director. The leader had clear leveling documents that showcased and described the tasks, activities, and behaviors at each level, making it easier for the director to also see the level at which they weren't operating.

CULTURAL IMPACT

You hear a lot of companies say they have a "no assholes" policy.

In my experience, that's a lot easier to say than it is to execute. For that reason, cultural impact is the third filter.

There are two team culture truisms:

- What gets recognized gets repeated.

- What's allowed is what persists.

I had a manager in my feedback training course who was struggling with a team member. This person was their top producer and by all accounts a very opinionated and difficult person to work with. New hires were scared of this person because asking a question of her often resulted in a condescending response.

The strategy within the organization to that point was to just wall her off: let her bring in the sales, flatter her to make her feel important, but shield her from everything else as best as possible. They allowed the bad behavior, and so it persisted.

Within the sales org, they talked about their values: teamwork, collaboration, and customer-first mentality. Yet, they had someone who everyone knew wasn't a good team member and didn't collaborate, so it was as if their values had a big asterisk: *"We expect everyone but her to live these values."*

It doesn't matter what you say you expect or the company values posters you put on the walls if the observed behaviors and attitudes are not aligned. It's those observed behaviors that are your real culture.

In these cases, your job is to ask these questions: *What's the message I'm sending by retaining this person? Is this a message that proudly reflects my team and culture?*

If you don't like your answers to those two honest questions, it might be time to consider parting ways.

Additionally, before you're in a tough spot with a particular employee, it's important to get clear and concise about the behaviors you will and won't tolerate. This is above and beyond your stated company values. This is one of the reasons the "no asshole" rule in many companies often fails. They don't preemptively take the time to identify what it means to be an "asshole," so those folks often persist because there's not a joint understanding or clear criteria for when one has crossed into that dreaded territory.

CHAPTER SUMMARY

Deciding whether and when to part ways with someone is a loaded decision that sits on the shoulders of managers, and knowing you're impacting someone's livelihood makes it even more challenging.

After twenty years of making hiring and firing decisions and working with hundreds of managers as they make these decisions, one thing stands out: the largest regret is often taking too long to make the decision.

Overwhelmingly, with the multitude of people I've let go over the years, the number-one reaction I've observed in them is relief. I gave them a fair shot, and they did their best; it just wasn't the right fit.

To help in your decision-making, practice these additional thought exercises:

1. **Rate of improvement**: Can their rate of growth keep up with the needs of the business?

2. **Operating level**: Is there alignment between how they are operating and the level of their role?

3. **Cultural impact**: What does it say about your culture if you retain this person?

BALANCING WHEN PERSONAL IMPACTS PROFESSIONAL

How do you manage performance when someone is going through a tough time personally? Can you still hold them to performance standards? Can you still give them feedback?

Here's how a manager typically poses it to me:

I need to address where they're missing, but I don't want to overburden them while they have so much going on.

I'm guessing, fabulous manager, you can empathize with this challenge.

This chapter will offer you a powerful consideration, real empowerment, and a path forward in these sticky situations.

A POWERFUL CONSIDERATION

Here's a simple, daring question: who on your team is fighting a silent battle?

Their child is being bullied. They have an addiction. Their marriage is falling apart. They've had a falling out with a family member.

The point is this: not everyone who is going through something tells us.

When considering whether, and how, to approach someone when they're going through a tough time, I ask myself these two questions:

- Should the person who has vocalized their battle be treated differently than someone suffering a silent battle?

- Should the person who has been vocal be held to different standards than the person who is more private?

This isn't about a right or wrong answer; it's about challenging our thinking.

When we reexamine the situation through this perspective, it's eye-opening and reframes the challenge at hand.

BE EMPOWERED

It's from managing people through deaths of loved ones, diagnoses of diseases, military deployments of spouses, divorces, and loss of children that my leadership mantra was born: Be Human, with Standards.

What does this mean in practice?

Someone's child is in the hospital. My human reaction? *"Go, leave, get to the hospital. Can I help you get there?"*

And when the hospital stay sadly extends longer than anticipated, having standards means we begin to have open and honest conversations about what is and is not possible during this time.

What this also means is an individual approach to management. I don't manage two people the same. I do hold them to the same standards, but how we get there is different.

When a team member is going through a tough time, I meet them with genuine care and empathy while honoring the standards of the team.

You should absolutely feel empowered to be the leader who is human and has standards. We live in the *and*, not the *or*. We don't have to sacrifice being human for standards, and having standards doesn't need to hinder our humanity.

YOUR PATHWAY FORWARD

You're reading this because you likely didn't receive a manual on how to have difficult conversations. You likely also didn't receive a roadmap and decision tree that would prepare you to know how to handle the challenge of simultaneously delivering for the business while navigating the curveballs of life.

This is the sticky stuff not enough people talk about. I hope this book changes that.

Here are helpful actions to take when the professional and personal collide.

1. PICK YOUR TIMING

Put this into the category of "obvious and worth mentioning."

They're signing off in order to take their parent to chemo treatment. Do they need feedback right then? Probably not.

This is a simple, friendly reminder that timing matters.

If there doesn't seem to be a good time because the sh*t really has hit the fan in their life, try to find the best of the challenging timing, and acknowledge it.

2. ASK THEM

So often we make assumptions. We assume they can't handle feedback. We assume the performance conversation will send them over the edge.

We fail to ask the simple question: *"While you're going through this tough time, what role are you wanting work to play?"*

I start with this question because a surprising number of us want work to be a good distraction while other things fall apart.

I remember my leader, Jami, asking me this when my dad died. She told me to take the time that I needed and then asked in what ways I saw work fitting in.

I wanted work to be my distraction, the place where I could, for eight hours, forget about my sadness. And I didn't want to be treated differently. I wanted to pretend that this segment of life was still steady.

Others might tell you that there is not a place for work fitting in right now (more on that below). Point being, don't assume, ask.

If they do see work as a necessary distraction, then ask:

> *I want to be sensitive to ebbs and flows of emotion as you're navigating this time. When I have coaching for you and feedback to help you within your role, in what ways would you like me to approach you differently than I have been?*

There might be no difference. They might want you to tee it up more with positivity. They might want you to hold all feedback until Thursday. Whatever it is, ask them.

3. REVISIT EXPECTATIONS

You've gotten their input on the role they want work to play during this time. Now it's helpful to revisit and update expectations.

Below are practical questions to support your efforts:

- Would it be helpful to keep or skip our one-to-one next week?

- Would you like to share this with the team or keep it private?

- What do we want to revisit about your measures of success?

- What adjustments do we want to our frequency of communication?

It might be that they ask for more frequent check-ins. They might indicate a desire for you to double-check things periodically. Whatever it is, the goal is to get things out on the table for stronger alignment, which connects back to the importance (and role) of Relationship in our Fearless Feedback Framework.

4. EXPLORE TEMPORARY SOLUTIONS

If what they're going through is so significant that they're unable to be at work, are highly distracted, or their output and contributions are struggling, it's fair to explore temporary solutions.

- Might a leave of absence be appropriate?

- Might a reduced schedule make sense?

- Might a part-time contractor help?

I was recently working with someone who experienced a pregnancy loss. Understandably, it impacted her work. She felt she had one foot at work, one leg knee deep trying to heal her body and soul.

She wanted to execute, and she wasn't. She knew it. She would've greatly appreciated the option of a leave.

Thinking in terms of acute — sudden and short-lived — or chronic and requiring longer term management and consideration is a valuable starting place.

Looking for creative solutions that meet both the needs of the human and the needs of the business is reasonable in these situations, and will require you to work with your leader and HR.

It's not to say there is always an easy remedy or that the requested accommodations are possible. Exploring possibilities can add another layer of challenge for you as you navigate processes and approvals with your HR business partners.

It is to say that if you don't ask, you don't get. Ask for help, ask for options, and see what's possible so you're not making assumptions. The answer might be no, but the answer could be yes.

CHAPTER SUMMARY

Managing performance during someone's personal struggles isn't about lowering the bar; it's about leading with humanity while holding to shared standards.

Here are your keys to success:

1. **Pick Your Timing**: Remember this in the heat of the moment.

2. **Ask Them**: Watch your assumptions, and ask about the role work plays during this time.

3. **Revisit Expectations**: Create strong alignment and clarity while they experience hardship.

4. **Explore Temporary Solutions**: Get creative and work with HR to understand what could be possible.

GIVING FEEDBACK TO REMOTE EMPLOYEES

If sharing feedback to remote employees feels challenging, you're not alone.

A *Harvard Business Review* survey (as reported by SHRM) found "40% of managers/supervisors had low confidence in their ability to manage remote workers.[9]"

What I hear from managers and is confirmed by reporting from SHRM is folks feel it's harder to read nuances or subtleties over a computer screen than when they're in person.

As a result, hybrid and remote employees receive less weekly feedback than on-site workers.

These findings further validate the importance of Fearless Feedback and how necessary it is to operate at the intersection of Mindset, Relationship, and Delivery.

9 Brian O'Connell and Electa Willander, "The Biggest Remote-Work Lessons Managers Have Learned," SHRM (2021)

MINDSET: CHALLENGE YOUR PERSPECTIVE

There's an exercise I do in live, virtual training with managers, and it's powerful in helping to refine perspectives on remote feedback.

A manager will comment on the difficulty of reading the room or reading someone's reaction over video. Each time this happens, I find myself giving a mischievous, broad smile.

I hear them out and recognize the concern as valid (which it is), and then we dive in.

First, I'll tell the group, *"Type into chat the emotion you see on my face right now."*

In that moment, I'm still holding my big grin. Everyone will type in words such as *happy, engaged,* or *joyful.*

Yes, perfect, they get it every time.

Then, I change my facial expression and instruct them to note in the chat how they'd describe my body language. Interestingly enough, they'll type in words that capture the message my face and body is sending.

We'll do it a third time with an updated expression, and again the group will identify it correctly.

At that point, I'll then say, *"What are you seeing through this exercise?"*

Each group I've ever done this with will come to this conclusion: it's not as hard as we tell ourselves to read someone over video conferencing.

The heart of it is this: when we're remote, we see the reactions; we just don't have the same level of courage to address them.

When we're in person, we tell ourselves it feels more natural to pause and address when someone's gone quiet or has a puzzled look on their face. When we engage virtually, acknowledging reactions may feel more confrontational, so we may doubt if it's okay to do so.

Here's the fascinating thing: managers often agonize over *how* to deliver feedback to a remote team member when the research points to a simpler truth. Gallup found that 8 in 10 employees who received meaningful feedback in the past week were fully engaged—nearly 4x the global average[10].

It's not the medium that moves the needle. It's the frequency; the High Cadence, Low Stakes concept I first introduced in Chapter 6.

The real barrier isn't the screen, it's our Mindset.

RELATIONSHIP: INCREASE INTENTIONALITY

It's absolutely true that in-person relationships can feel easier to grow and maintain than virtual relationships.

This is in part due to the casual nature in which we can engage throughout the day when someone is in our same office: those smiles and quick greetings as you pass in the hall or the quick brainstorming that happens on the heels of asking someone about their weekend.

In Daniel Coyle's *The Culture Code: The Secrets of Highly Successful Groups*[11], he tells us about the culture at Zappos and how their CEO focused on creating "collisions," which are "serendipitous personal encounters" that are the lifeblood of any organization as they are "drivers of creativity, community, and cohesion."

In person, we rely on these "collisions" to help us with our relationships. As a result, we can take for granted and become more lazy in fostering our connections. Managing remote workers requires us to be more intentional and aware of how,

10 Jim Harter, "What to Ask the Hybrid and Remote Workforce," Gallup (2023)

11 Daniel Coyle, *The Culture Code: The Secrets of Highly Successful Groups*, (New York, Bantam Books, 2018), page 66.

when, and where we're investing in relationship dynamics with our team.

This is why casual, friendly pings, quality one-to-one meetings, regular phone calls, and more are fundamental to your mutual success. It's very easy for these relationships to become highly transactional by only reaching out when you need something from one another. Our task is to ensure we don't fall into that trap and consciously and intentionally invest time and energy into staying connected.

Below are a few ideas for how to be even more intentional with remote relationship-building:

- **Have Relationship Kickoff Conversations**: Discuss what's important to each of you in how you stay connected remotely.

- **Host whiteboarding sessions**: Mimic the benefits of in-person brainstorms with intentional sessions by video call.

- **Have fun**: Send a funny (work-appropriate) gif or meme to share simple laughs.

- **Include icebreakers**: Kick off team meetings with personal shares and lighthearted questions.

- **Host end-of-week wrap-ups**: Share shoutouts, upcoming action items, and even a highlight and learning moment of the week.

- **Follow up**: When they share life events, follow up with interest in how things went.

- **Use names**: Use the names of the important people in their life, as opposed to *"how are your kids?"*

DELIVERY: USE MEANINGFUL TRANSITIONS

Getting into a real-time coaching or feedback conversation with someone who is remote typically has three entry points:

- DM to ask them to hop on a call.

- Request they stick around after a group call.

- Start a conversation in their one-to-one meeting.

There's good news. The core features of a strong Transition (focusing on their self-interest, leading with good intent, and asking permission) all apply to feedback for remote employees.

DM TO GET ON A CALL

When you need to ping your team member to ask if they hop on a call, the Headline you've prepared for your conversation can serve as your DM.

These examples strike the right balance of giving them a heads-up of what you'll be talking about without them freaking out and reading too much into your tone or message:

- Hello! Any chance you have a few minutes to hop on the phone now? I have a few ideas to elevate the messaging in your deck, and think it will help strengthen your position in tomorrow's meeting with the product team. Want to give me a call?

- Hey there! Might you have ten minutes later today? I'm hoping to connect on something I'm seeing that I believe will be important for how you're developing in your career, and it's within the topic of collaboration. Nothing scary, I promise. :)

What you want to avoid is this: *"Hey! Do you have a few min-utes to hop on a call?*

You've likely received that type of ping, and even though your rational mind knows that nothing is wrong, you likely wondered, *"Oh no, what did I do?"*

Avoid creating that type of panic with your people by shar-ing a wee bit of context for your request on their time. A well-crafted Headline can help.

REQUESTING THEY STICK AROUND

Now imagine you're wrapping up a team meeting, and you're wanting one team member to stay on the call for coaching or feedback.

The key is to casually dismiss everyone else while warmly calling on the person you'd like to remain on the line. Here's how that might sound:

- Thanks everyone! Hey, Hannah, could you hang back? I'd love to connect on the project on your plate right now.

- I appreciate everyone's time today, thank you. Joe, before you hang up, could I steal five minutes of your time? I've got an idea that could help with one of your stakeholders.

Once you've got them in a one-to-one setting, you can thank them for joining you and then dive into the conversation.

ADDRESSING IN
THEIR ONE-TO-ONE MEETING

The last common scenario for feedback sharing with remote folks is in their one-to-one meeting.

Ideally, in the Relationship Kickoff Conversation, you had an opportunity to discuss timing and delivery preferences as a remote employee. They might prefer to see the feedback as an agenda item, so they aren't surprised. They might request you send high-level feedback topics ahead of time.

If they don't have particular preferences, view the virtual one-to-one meeting as you would in person. It's your chance to connect personally, discuss growth, prioritize development, and increase alignment. In person, you'd launch into the feedback by starting with your Headline; the same is true for remote feedback interactions.

CHAPTER SUMMARY

It's tempting to tell ourselves that we can't give feedback as well to our remote employees. The reality is it simply takes greater intentionality and a healthy dose of courage.

- **Mindset**: Challenge your perspective and limiting beliefs about remote feedback. Remember: Your people *want* your coaching and development.

- **Relationship**: Increase your intentionality when you're remote by consciously investing time and effort into strong relationships.

- **Delivery**: Use meaningful transitions to ensure we're bringing up coaching and feedback in a way that prioritizes their goals and aspirations.

MAXIMIZING POSITIVE FEEDBACK

I've defined feedback as information that helps someone be their best. Feedback is at the heart of managing performance, developing careers, and engaging our people, and positive feedback is essential in these efforts.

As I mentioned in the Introduction, the proportion of critical feedback discussed in this book is not indicative of positive feedback being less important. In fact, it's arguably more impactful.

Positive feedback (appreciation and recognition) reinforces great performance and behaviors, builds confidence, increases retention, and is often underutilized by managers.

Consider these powerful data points from Gallup[12]:

---

12 "The Importance of Employee Recognition: Low Cost, High Impact," Gallup, 2024, https://www.gallup.com/workplace/236441/employee-recognition-low-cost-high-impact.aspx

- Only one in three workers in the US strongly agrees they have received recognition or praise for doing good work in the past seven days.

- Employees who do not feel adequately recognized are 2x as likely to say they'll quit in the next year.

When I talk with managers about the need for positive feedback, there's a consistent reaction: *I know I should, and I always forget.*

We don't intentionally fail to deliver on the volume of positive feedback our people need. We're so overloaded with putting out fires and managing day-to-day efforts that we put appreciation and recognition on the back burner.

Let me suggest ways to both build your positive feedback practice and help you get the most bang for your buck.

APPRECIATION VS. RECOGNITION

You have two powerful tools at your disposal for increasing the positive reinforcement you're giving your people: appreciation and recognition.

Appreciation	Recognition
Highlighting *who* the are.	Celebrating *what* they did.
Character inputs.	Actionable outputs.

The area you're likely stronger in is recognition: when someone hits a goal or delivers a project, you likely acknowledge the effort.

And there's space to take things further.

We want to recognize the inputs, not just the outputs.

Here are three samples of appreciation:

- I'm so grateful you're on this team. You bring a level of calm and creative troubleshooting when we're putting out a fire, and I value you immensely.

- I have to tell you how much I value you. Your thoughtful communication and how you're able to zoom out with a broader perspective are two really impactful ways you're modeling excellence within this team. Thank you!

- I'm not sure I communicate how much I value you enough! You're steady and an utter joy to work with, and you help us all be better. We're so lucky to have you!

Notice the attributes of their character that are called out in the examples above: *calm, creative, thoughtful communication, broader perspective, steady, an utter joy.*

When we acknowledge what we see and the extent to which we value that quality, we increase the probability that they will continue exhibiting that behavior. What gets recognized gets repeated.

What I also value about delineating between appreciation and recognition is that when we celebrate the right behaviors, the desired inputs and preferred ways of engaging, we also end up having fewer difficult feedback conversations about behavior that needs changing.

You already know how to praise an accomplishment, which is recognition. Let me also remind you of the value of specificity.

"Good work on that project," doesn't hit the same way as, *"I want to thank you for the way you organized that project, and I want to commend you for your continued efforts when things got tough."*

Similarly, *"Great communication plan!"* is a quick moment of recognition that could be even more memorable to your team member by saying, *"I really admire the way you designed the communication plan for this rollout. You executed flawlessly, thank you."*

Being specific with appreciation and recognition also extends to engaging with your peers and your own manager.

Imagine your manager forwards you a heads-up of what's happening in another part of the business. When you receive it, you can reply with one of these two options:

- Thanks so much for forwarding this my way. Seeing what's coming down the pike is super valuable to me, and I appreciate you looping me in.

- Thank you again for keeping me in the know about adjustments to engineering's timelines. I really value you trusting me with this information.

By replying with positive reinforcement, you're letting your manager know how much you value the action they've taken, increasing the likelihood they continue to do it.

COMMON MANAGER QUESTION

I'm often asked, *"How much positive reinforcement do I really need to give?"*

The short answer is this: more than you think.

From a performance angle, a study shared by *Harvard Business Review*[13] found the following:

- Highest-performing teams averaged ~5.6 positive comments for every negative.

- Medium-performing team averaged ~1.9:1.

- Low-performing teams averaged ~.36:1 (more negative than positive).

Then there's the engagement perspective.

Research from Gallup and Workhuman "confirms that frequent recognition amplifies the impact of frequent feedback. Among employees who report receiving feedback and recognition from their manager at least once a week, 61% are engaged. These employees are significantly more likely to be engaged than employees who receive feedback from their manager at least once a week but receive recognition less often (38%).[14]"

Your first step to boost your ratio of positive to critical feedback is practicing looking for the good.

Look for your people doing the right thing. Look for your people demonstrating creativity. Look for instances of independence and impactful decision-making.

When I was working to build this muscle, I created weekly calendar reminders for myself. For fifteen minutes on Wednesday and Friday mornings, I'd pause and think about what I saw

---

13 Jack Zenger and Joseph Folkman, "The Ideal Praise to Criticism Ratio," Harvard Business Review, 2013.

14 "Organizations Can Redefine Feedback by Including Recognition," Gallup, 2024, https://www.gallup.com/workplace/651812/organizations-redefine-feedback-including-recognition.aspx.

over the previous days. And then I'd queue up appreciation and recognition.

Sometimes I sent an immediate ping to the person to express my gratitude. Other times I put it on our one-to-one meeting agenda to share directly. I've also been known to mail a thank-you card to the home of a remote employee.

When you look for the good, you'll find it. Then you can intentionally highlight inputs, not just outputs.

CHAPTER SUMMARY

You can move the needle on performance, development, and engagement when you invest in your practice of positive reinforcement. These conversations are not nearly as stressful or loaded, so entire books aren't written about them. However, they're an important practice of being a great manager.

Below are two key ways to think about positive feedback:

- **Appreciation**: Communicate *who* you see and the ways in which you value these attributes.

- **Recognition**: Highlight *what* someone has done, with specificity.

APPROACHING FEEDBACK FOR YOUR MANAGER AND PEERS

Giving upward and peer feedback can be stressful. We can easily talk ourselves out of having the conversation. After all, these folks don't report to us, and we're not responsible for their growth and results. How they're seen within the business doesn't impact us to the same degree as someone on our team.

There's good news! The principles you've learned so far can be leveraged here, with some bonus methods to set you up for success.

UPWARD FEEDBACK

Upward feedback is the sharing of feedback with someone more senior than you in the org chart. For our purposes, I'll focus on the most common form: feedback shared with your manager or leader.

This flavor of feedback also happens to be an evergreen topic within one-to-one coaching sessions. I have three favorite tactics that resonate with my clients, and I hope they resonate with you as well.

Upward feedback has such a wide spectrum: from NBD (no big deal) because you've got a great history and relationship with your leader to crazy tough for a whole slew of reasons.

When it comes to these feedback conversations, power dynamics and your previous experiences giving upward feedback can impact your level of comfort. Your leader may also send a signal that upward feedback is encroaching onto enemy territory.

All of this can be true, *and* if the situation is taking up mental space and/or impacting the way we engage, we want to be able to say confidently that we did everything within our power to positively impact the situation.

Our first step is to ensure we're rooted in our Fearless Feedback Framework.

Start with Mindset. What's your current mindset about approaching your leader?

If you notice your mind is assuming the worst, the Chapter 2 strategy of reanchoring to the middle case can serve you well here. Notice any worst-case assumptions, and then consciously bring to mind the most probable middle case.

With someone with whom the reporting relationship is relatively new, it can be helpful to adopt this mindset: *I have an insight that will help them to help me.*

From that perspective, it can feel less daunting. Step powerfully into the mindset that will serve you best.

Relationship, especially with upward feedback, is a *key* driver. When I've surveyed participants in my live feedback courses about the ease with which they give their manager feedback, overwhelmingly, those who have a solid and open relationship have no problem sharing feedback. Unfortunately, that seems to be the exception as opposed to the rule.

If you're in the camp of wishing you had a better relationship with your manager, or your experiences with them cause concerns about how your message will be received, the immediate action is to lean into Relationship. Start by thinking about how you can create trust and safety through your tone, body language, and approach.

The longer term action with Relationship is to ensure you drive the Relationship Kickoff Conversation with every new manager you report into. That conversation with your manager can create a more solid foundation to approach upward feedback in the future.

Below are helpful questions you can leverage in upward Relationship Kickoff Conversations:

- When I identify ways I believe you can help me further unlock my potential and impact, what's your preference for how I approach you?

- As we begin working together, I assume I might have ideas or suggestions that might help you as you're managing all of us. At those points, what are your preferences for how I share those ideas?

For Delivery, the last component of Fearless Feedback, I have three strategies that continue to leverage your Headline,

Observation, Ask framework. These tactics can be mixed and matched, used independently, or used together within one conversation.

TACTIC 1: SHARE YOUR SELF-REALIZATION

This first approach is to let your leader in on something you're realizing about yourself and then ask for their help.

Let's pretend your leader is constantly seven to ten minutes late to your one-to-one meetings, and it makes you feel he doesn't respect your time. Each time it happens, it bothers you more and more because you've got loads of other things you'd rather be doing than sitting on a call waiting for his arrival.

In this case, you're associating being late with him lacking respect for you, and it's really starting to push your buttons.

Try this in your next one-to-one meeting:

Headline

I'm wondering if I can share something that I'm starting to really realize about myself, and it relates to our one-to-one meetings.

Observation

I'm realizing how much I value time: being on time, using time wisely, and wrapping up on time. I'm noticing when our one-to-one meetings start late, I start to feel I'm losing time or am not being efficient with my time.

Ask

Something I've identified that would help me is if you give me a heads-up if you think you might be running late. With a heads-up, I could stay focused on what I'm working on and then join the call when you're ready. Is that something you could help me with?

This tactic can be helpful if you're worried about your leader being defensive or not receiving feedback well. Here's why it's effective:

- You're not pointing the finger of blame.

- You're making it about you, not them.

- You're suggesting a solution or action.

TACTIC 2: SHARE HOW YOU'RE RECEIVING THEIR ACTION

This approach is about sharing how you're perceiving, or receiving, an action they take.

Let's pretend your manager is micromanaging you on a new project. It's a change of course from the way they typically engage with you and your work. The level of questions and involvement from her makes you feel she doesn't trust you or your decision-making.

So try this . . .

Headline

I'm wanting to connect with you on X project. I know it's super important to you and our Q3 results. Might you have five minutes for me today?

Observation

I'm noticing you're engaging on a much deeper level than you have on previous projects, and the way I'm receiving it is you're questioning my judgment driving this project forward. I thought it was worth bringing up, so we can both feel positioned to deliver great results.

[They respond with something like, *"No, I'm not meaning to,"* or *"No, you're doing a great job, but . . . "*]

Ask

That's fair. I didn't believe you were intending to have me feel this way. What I'd propose is we chat through some ideas for what I could do to proactively ensure you have all the details you need, so we strike a balance of me still feeling empowered and trusted and you having easy access to what you need. Could we chat through and problem-solve?

This approach can work well when you have a history with your leader and can be more candid. Hearing how you're *receiving* their action can be the tiny jolt they might need to understand how their actions are being interpreted.

TACTIC 3: LEADING WITH VULNERABILITY

I first learned about Vulnerability Loops reading Daniel Coyle's *Culture Code.* It goes like this:

Person 1 says something vulnerable, admitting a sentiment, mistake, or shortcoming.

Person 2 receives the vulnerability as a signal of trust. (*"They trust me enough to be open."*)

Person 2 becomes more willing and engaged, sending back a trust signal.

Person 1 feels more psychologically safe, so a candid exchange can ensue.

As managers and leaders, we should be leading with vulnerability first and often.

Vulnerability may not be a natural state for you, and that's okay. It's a muscle you can build that deepens connections and communication. In its simplest form, it's a willingness to be our authentic selves, admit our limitations, and acknowledge uncertainties.

When you need to share upward feedback and feel cautious, concerned, or unsure of how they'll respond, leading with vulnerability in your Headline can be an impactful approach to keep the walls of defensiveness low while sending a signal to kick off an open exchange.

Here's how it can sound in practice.

Let's pretend you've recently had a performance review with your manager, and you were surprised by both your rating and one area of development. It felt like it was a bit of a punch to the gut because it was feedback you hadn't heard before.

Here's how you can use Vulnerability (tactic 3) and Receiving (tactic 2) together to approach your leader:

Headline

I want to own up to being nervous about bringing this up. I'm wondering if we could revisit our last conversation about my development. Could we spend a few minutes on that?

Observation

After thinking more about it, the way I experienced the conversation was I found it to be surprising and disappointing. Reflecting deeper, what I realized is it was the surprise element that really got me.

Ask

I have an idea for both an ask and a commitment. First, could I ask that you add feedback onto our meeting agenda? I'd always much rather know than not know. And then I'd propose that I commit to asking for more feedback, so we can meet in the middle. This way I don't feel surprised if I miss the mark. Would you be open to that?

By opening your Headline with naming how you're feeling (nervous, in this example), your leader's brain is going to tell them, *"Hey, they're about to open up. Don't make them more nervous, and be sure to hear them out."*

Good leaders will hear this message and use it as a launching pad to have an open dialogue about how to exchange feedback and what they can do to help you feel less nervous in the future.

Leaders still developing their management effectiveness are less likely to take that extra step. They will typically put their guard down to hear you and simply acknowledge what you've shared.

COMMON MANAGER QUESTION

If you're in a tough spot with your current manager and thinking, *"What if my manager has a pattern of penalizing people who give them feedback,"* you're not alone.

It hurts my heart each time I work with someone who shares stories of their manager behaving this way.

Below are a few options:

- **Additional support**: Do you have a friendly and productive relationship with either their boss or your HR business partner? Might you approach them for guidance? Share that you're really wanting to solve it directly with your manager and that you'd value any input they might have that could help you land your message.

- **Master your assumptions**: Double-check that your fears and assumptions are the middle case, not the worst case. Look for evidence to confirm your

assumptions or reject any false narratives. You want
to check the box that your Mindset isn't setting you
up to fail or going into overdrive, preventing you
from approaching the conversation.

- **Evaluate the ROI**: Pretend for a moment you're
  right, that folks who give your manager feedback
  face repercussions. What's the ROI on having the
  conversation? Is the topic consequential enough
  that it's worth approaching? Remember the
  concept of clearing the air (Chapter 9). If you're
  proud of how you've shown up and how you've
  attempted to be an effective manager within
  the team, then there might be a case for trying
  to let it roll off your back. In those cases, what I
  tell myself is this: *they're making choices I wouldn't
  make, and that gets to be okay.* That thought lets me
  sleep well at night when I determine the ROI on a
  conversation with someone more senior to me is
  not worth it.

PEER-TO-PEER FEEDBACK

Similar to upward feedback, our ease and comfort sharing
feedback with peers and cross-functional partners is directly
correlated to the quality and depth of our relationship with
them.

For that reason, I emphasize the importance of both the
Relationship Kickoff Conversation and Relationship Reinvestment Conversations with the folks who don't report to you
but whose actions and behaviors impact your work.

Here are a few questions that can be helpful as you establish
and maintain relationships around the business:

- Because we both can be moving a million miles a minute, I'd propose we openly chat through what changes we can make in how we communicate when we're under stress. I'll share first . . . for me, I have a tendency to _____. What are things I should look out for so that a) I don't take anything personally, and b) I can offer support?

- It's bound to happen that folks on my team will approach me with feedback for you and your team. I want to be sure to handle those scenarios as best as possible. What would be helpful for us to align on before that happens?

- It's also fair to say we'll likely have points where we're either competing for resources or have a difference of opinion. If and when that happens, how do we want to work through it together?

In my experience, most frustrations and therefore feedback situations with peers or cross-functional partners, come from lacking mutual clarity and a safe environment to communicate directly and with care with the other person.

When we establish and align on communication norms from the get-go and then periodically check in to make adjustments, we make our lives easier. This highlights the importance of Relationship Banking.

Relationship Banking is the notion that you can and should be making frequent, meaningful deposits in your relationships around the business. At different junctions, you're going to need to make a withdrawal (asking them for help, requesting they deprioritize something, etc), a withdrawal should always leave a balance in the bank. No negative balances here.

From this lens, we can then view peer-to-peer feedback as a valuable deposit into our relationship bank account.

We do this by thinking about the feedback not as feedback but rather as an offering with partnership.

This is the Mindset I step into: *I have an idea to offer that I believe will make life easier.*

All of a sudden, that shift in perspective lowers my heart rate as I begin to craft my Delivery.

Let me use Headline, Observation, Ask to model two versions of this mentality.

EXAMPLE 1: DEVELOPMENT OPPORTUNITY VIA OFFERING

Imagine you're in a meeting, and your peer is trying to gain buy-in for their proposal. You watch them get a bit flustered, and the decision-makers on the call kindly but clearly keep the meeting agenda going without affirmation or next steps to your peer's presentation.

Headline

I'm wondering if we could connect for a few minutes. I have a couple of ideas that could be helpful as you're gaining buy-in for the redesign project. Do you have a few minutes now?

Observation

When you did your run-through, I noticed some of the questions seemed to throw you off and spark a bit of frustration or defensiveness of the ideas. What was it like for you?

Ask

I've definitely been there. It's not easy. What I thought I'd offer is the idea of selling the problem first. Your ideas are solid, and if you were to connect them to the problem and help everyone experience the challenge, you'll have an easier time gaining buy-in and likely won't be back on your heels when answering questions.

This person doesn't report to you, and now you're meeting them with an offer of an idea after seeing them struggle in a meeting. They can take it or leave it. What I hope you also noticed was the question in there: *What was it like for you?* As a peer, you can be a powerful sounding board for their growth, and there's a decent chance they'll open up to you more than their manager.

EXAMPLE 2: IMPROVING COMMUNICATION VIA MUTUAL SUCCESS

This next example is for the instance where your communication with a partner is off. Your frustration is mounting because you're not getting what you need. You've identified that your mutual success is at risk, and therefore, it's time to open up a dialogue to explore.

Headline

Hey, friend . . . I'm hoping the two of us can revisit our communication flow to help us avoid hurdles as we dive into Q2 planning and prioritization. Do you have a few minutes?

Observation

When we're knee-deep in things, I've noticed that the volume of our communication sometimes decreases, and I'm realizing it's making me feel a bit in the dark.

Ask

I know we're both moving super fast, and I think we'll be set up for greater mutual benefit if we pause for a minute to figure out the cadence that enables both of us to feel successful. Are you open to chatting through what's working and what could be better in our information sharing?

You'll notice a few things:

- We're carrying over the self-realization tactic we used with upward feedback.

- The focus is on "we," not "you."

- You're focusing on your mutual benefit and success.

CHAPTER SUMMARY

You can be effective with upward and peer feedback using the same Fearless Feedback Framework and HOA framework discussed throughout the book.

In the case of upward feedback, you now have these in your back pocket for your Delivery:

1. Sharing your self-realization

2. Sharing how you're receiving their action

3. Leading with vulnerability

Peer feedback can go more smoothly when you consider positioning your message as an offering and/or an opportunity for mutual success.

ASKING (AND GETTING) VALUABLE FEEDBACK FROM OTHERS

Envision this . . . You're wrapping up a one-to-one meeting with a relatively new team member, and you ask, *"Do you have any feedback for me? Anything I could be doing better in managing you?"*

What do you bet the response is more than 90% of the time?

You guessed it: *"Not that I can think of!"*

Maybe you're relieved; after all, you asked the question, and they had a chance to speak up. Maybe you're a little frustrated. I mean, how can you be a stronger manager if they don't let you know how you're doing?

Now think back to the times you've experienced this with

your own managers. You probably asked the questions: *"How am I doing? Anything I could be doing better?"*

And you likely got a version of this: *"You're doing great. Keep up the good work."*

In those moments, you might have thought, *"Great, no news is good news."* Or, you might have felt disappointed, wishing you had gotten more coaching and feedback from your manager.

Wherever you land on the reaction spectrum for these common scenarios, there are three reasons you're not getting valuable feedback:

1. Their previous experience has taught them not to speak up.

2. Your ask is too broad.

3. "Feedback" freaks people out.

THEIR PREVIOUS EXPERIENCE

Particularly for those folks who report to you, their experiences may have taught them not to give feedback to their manager.

Perhaps a family member taught them to just keep their head down, do the work, and not rock the boat. Perhaps they've had a manager in a former role who taught them a harsh lesson, and they felt the repercussions of speaking up.

So, what can you do?

Get curious about their lived experience with upward feedback.

I highlighted this earlier in the Relationship Kickoff Conversation, and it's important to revisit now.

In the scope of that foundational conversation, it might sound like this:

> *I'm interested in better understanding your experience with upward feedback. I ask because it's important for me to grow and adjust to be the best manager for you that I can be. I'd like to be able to ask for your input on how I can be a better manager and leader for you. So, what's been your experience sharing upward feedback in the past?*

This next part is really important.

After you ask the question and they share their previous experience, these are the next two words that need to come out of your mouth: *"Thank you."*

> *Thank you for sharing . . .*
>
> *Thank you for trusting me with what your experience has been . . .*

You have an opportunity right here to send a powerful signal of trust. Thanking them immediately increases the likelihood that they will feel you to be a safe space to openly communicate.

YOUR ASK IS TOO BROAD

Asking, *"Do you have any feedback for me,"* is too broad. It's like looking at the menu at The Cheesecake Factory. Where do you look first? If you're like me, it's overwhelming, so I don't even bother.

That's what's happening when you ask broadly for feedback.

Instead, let's help others and ourselves by reducing the scope of our ask and getting more specific.

Are you looking for feedback on your communication with

stakeholders? Your progress in leadership presence? The one or two blind spots that might hinder your growth?

Specific asks get specific answers.

Try these more specific questions with those you manage:

- If there were one thing I could do better to help you succeed, what would that be?

- Thinking about how I communicate updates to you and the team, what's an idea you have that would improve the quality of my communication?

- My goal is to be a manager who invests in the development of my people. What's a suggestion you might offer me to help you feel stronger career development?

Each of these questions can and should be followed with open and unattached curiosity. As you discuss, don't be afraid to continue to follow up using the best question of all: *What else?*

Thinking about getting better feedback from your leader, consider these sample questions:

- I'm wanting to make sure I stay on a solid path for my development, especially with my executive communication. What one or two ideas might you have that would help me be even more effective with my comms?

- As you know, earning a promotion to director is my next career milestone. I'm wondering whether I can ask for your advice. Knowing me and my work, what one or two suggestions would you have to ensure I'm keeping my trajectory and moving my development forward?

 I've put together an initial plan for how and where
I think I can continue growing and developing
within this team and org. I've self-identified three
core areas, and I'd value your input. What are
you seeing that would strengthen what I've
put together?

Here's a pro tip: give folks a heads-up.

This is an email I've actually sent. You can see that I've bulleted out a few feedback questions for Jonathan. Part of what can hinder folks sharing thoughtful feedback is they haven't had time to think about it.

Consider sending this a few days before a planned meeting to give them space to think.

This Week's 1:1

Katie O'Brien Ceccarini
to me

Hey Jonathan!

For this week's 1:1, in addition to what we have on our agenda, I'd love if you came with some thoughts on the following:

- What could I be doing differently to ensure you're feeling fully supported and successful?
- On a scale of 1 to 10, I'd love for you to rate how well I communicate with you and anything you'd like to see me do differently.
- Anything else to help me to help you?

Looking forward to our 1:1!

Here's what to flag as you adopt this approach.

About 75% of the time, my folks would reply with their responses, but I wanted to be able to talk about it.

When I'd get the email response, I'd reply thanking them and saying that I'm looking forward to chatting further in our one-to-one meeting.

My reasoning is this: I want and need to build trust and safety that these conversations aren't scary. I recognize many folks feel better putting pen to paper to capture their thoughts, which is fantastic, and we also want to build a relationship where candid and honest conversations are foundational to our mutual growth.

"FEEDBACK" FREAKS PEOPLE OUT

As we established within the Headline, most people experience panic or dread when they hear, *"Can I give you some feedback?"*

It's also true when folks are being asked to give "feedback." The word creates a sense of confrontation, inadequacy, and worry about whether the person wants to hear the truth.

In fact, the American Psychological Association researched this. I particularly like this quote from *"Just Letting You Know" Underestimating Others' Desire for Constructive Feedback*[15]:

"People sometimes avoid giving feedback to others even when it would help fix others' problems. For example, only 2.6% of individuals in a pilot field study provided feedback to a survey administrator who had food or lipstick on their face. Five experiments (N = 1,984) identify a possible reason for the lack of feedback: people

---

15 Nicole Abi-Esber, et al. "'Just Letting You Know . . .' Underestimating Others' Desire for Constructive Feedback," *Journal of Personality and Social Psychology: Interpersonal Relations and Group Processes* (2022), https://doi.org/10.1037/pspi0000393

underestimate how much others want to receive constructive feedback."

You might have noticed that in the examples above, the word *feedback* was not used.

Instead, the following words were used:

- Ideas

- Input

- Advice

- Suggestions

It's not just my two decades of doing this work that has taught me that asking for ideas and advice yields more actionable results. *Harvard Business Review* shared the following in their article *"Why Asking for Advice Is More Effective Than Asking for Feedback"*[16]:

"Conventional wisdom says you should ask your colleagues for feedback. However, research suggests that feedback often has no (or even a negative) impact on our performance. This is because the feedback we receive is often too vague; it fails to highlight what we can improve on or how to improve.

Our latest research suggests a better approach. Across four experiments—including a field experiment conducted in an executive education classroom—we found that people received more effective input when they asked for advice rather than feedback."

16 Jaewon Yoon, et al. "Why Asking for Advice Is More Effective Than Asking for Feedback," *Harvard Business Review* (2019)

Now let me add one big caveat: the power and scariness of the word *feedback* diminishes as you have more trusting experiences and adopt a mindset (and create a team culture) of High Cadence, Low Stakes.

I briefly highlighted this concept back in Chapter 6 when looking at an example of Instance feedback. When we share coaching and real-time feedback at a high enough cadence, delivering feedback begins to feel low stakes.

There were folks on my teams to whom I could say, *"Hey, I'd love feedback on how I'm doing,"* and they'd feel more than comfortable having that dialogue with me. But it was a process, a journey, and for the sake of this book, I want to give you the most effective starting place. It starts with building the muscle to ask with greater specificity, so you get more specific responses in return.

CHAPTER SUMMARY

Your ability to get valuable feedback from those around you can be impacted by the following:

- Their previous experience

- Your ask being too broad

- Fears associated with the word *feedback*

To balance these out so you gain the insights that help you grow in your craft and career, adopt the following best practices:

1. Get curious about their experience during your Relationship Kickoff Conversation.

2. Ask specific questions, so you can get specific answers.

3. Use words such as *input, advice, suggestions,* or *recommendations* rather than *feedback.*

RECEIVING FEEDBACK EFFECTIVELY

Over the years, many companies have asked me to train their folks to receive feedback better. In every single case, after a consultative process, we've ended up doing two things: training the managers and training the individuals.

Why?

It's not 100% on the receiver to ensure the feedback is received well.

Philosophically, this is my belief: the giver and receiver each have a role to play.

That's one of the reasons I felt compelled to write this book. With more managers having the tools and the confidence to share feedback in a meaningful way, we'll put less pressure on the rest of the population to bear the full burden of receiving it well.

With that said, we have a responsibility to do what we can to receive feedback productively.

I have five techniques that can help. Choose the ones that will serve you best for where you are right now. Then come back to these in the future to reevaluate your needs.

1. Understand your tendencies.

2. Thank, Own, Ask.

3. Master your mindset.

4. Take some; leave some.

5. Choose your Being and Doing.

1. UNDERSTAND YOUR TENDENCIES

We're all wired for natural tendencies in response to challenging, tough, or surprising messages.

For me, my natural tendency is to feel defensive, and what comes out of my mouth are explanations for my confusion, the decision, and the gap being highlighted.

Viewing the most common natural tendencies as a staircase, what step do you most identify with as your immediate reaction? Without self-judgment, point to it:

Natural Tendencies

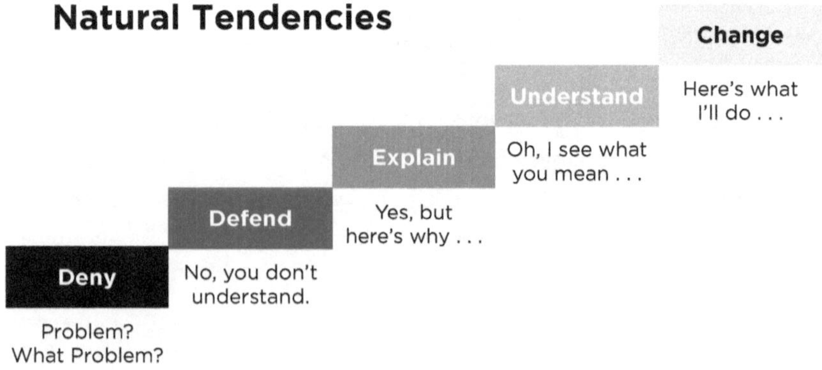

We cannot improve the way we receive feedback if we are not first honest about and aware of our natural tendencies.

Here's your key: identify what helps you move up the staircase.

In my early career, I lived between Defend and Explain for days. Through self-awareness and practice, I still land on Defend as my immediate reaction, but I now can move myself up to Change within moments.

The difference has largely stemmed from being able to manage up to my leaders to help them know my preferences.

Here's what I communicate to my manager about how I like to receive feedback:

- I don't like surprises. If you have feedback for me, add it to our one-to-one meeting agenda. I might see it and stress about it for a day or two, living in curiosity for what it all means and how the conversation will go. I much prefer that to being caught off guard that you have feedback for me.

- Assume good intent. I receive feedback really well when I feel that my manager knows that if I had a shortcoming, it wasn't for lack of effort or a desire to do well.

Similar to asking for feedback, when we share our preferences with specificity, we're helping others to help us.

Will you take a moment to identify what's important to you about how feedback is shared with you?

As you saw when we dug into the Relationship Kickoff Conversation, think about examples. Reflect on a time when you received constructive feedback and handled it well. How was it delivered? What felt different about this example compared to a time when you didn't handle it as well?

Write it down and have it ready to share with your manager.

2. THANK, OWN, ASK

This is a simple framework to help you in the moment of receiving difficult feedback.

Thank them for sharing.

Own up to your reaction.

Ask for what you need and then get curious.

Imagine you're in a meeting with your manager, and they give you feedback that the work you did on a key initiative didn't quite hit their expectations. You immediately start to feel frustration because the guidance wasn't clear, and you did your very best, tried to ask for help, and wish you'd known you were off track much earlier.

Here's how Thank, Own, Ask can come into play:

Thank

Thank you for letting me know where things fell short.

Own

I have to own up to how I'm feeling. I'm noticing frustration rising, and I don't want it to get the better of me.

Ask

Can you let me take a breather for just a couple of minutes? That'll help me stay open, and then I want to better understand where I missed and what I can do moving forward.

Put your manager hat back on. I'm guessing if your team member did this with you—thanked you for bringing it up, admitted what was happening internally, and asked for a hot second to compose themselves—you'd be more than willing to support and honor their request. Of course you would!

Give yourself the permission to use this as well.

3. MASTER YOUR MINDSET

Mindset plays a role in everything we do. Your inner game drives your outer game.

If your inner narratives start running off the rails, you're more likely to exhibit panic and stress externally. Then flip that around. When you're internally genuinely curious, your body language will shift, and you'll send a message of curiosity and interest.

To help me settle in with the right mindset, I challenge myself with these questions:

- What assumptions am I making?

- What insecurities is this feedback tapping into?

- What perspective will better serve me in this moment?

What's a mindset question you want to adopt for these moments? Can you write it down in a visible place near your desk? Until it's a stronger muscle, the visual cue will help.

4. TAKE SOME; LEAVE SOME

Not *all* feedback is a gift. And not *all* feedback has to be implemented.

Tough feedback can cause us to spiral, dwell, or have a thorn in our side. We have a choice to make, a discernment process to follow.

These two questions can help you determine the extent to which you want to implement the feedback you've received:

1. In what ways will this feedback serve my future self?

2. To what extent does this feedback align with where
   I want to take my career?

In Chapter 7, I shared a story of my own internal experience of feedback compared to the external display of emotion. In that moment, when Bridget told me how my peers were perceiving me (as defensive), it sucked. It stung like I cannot describe. Did I recognize that the feedback was going to serve my future self? Absolutely. Did her feedback align with how and where I wanted to take my career? 100%.

I've spent years building my skills and ways of thinking to not be perceived as a defensive team member. That feedback truly was a gift.

I was also told to tone down my energy. Was that feedback going to serve my future self? Not really. Was it aligned with the career I was building? Not at all. I'm not trying to attract super serious folks as you can tell from how I've written this book. I want to be real and truly me. That is feedback I chose not to implement. In fact, overwhelmingly, the most positive feedback I get from companies is about how I make their manager training engaging. It's my superpower.

To showcase another way of thinking about taking or leaving feedback, I'd like to highlight brilliance from an author I admire. Tara Mohr published *Playing Big* in 2014, and she teaches a key concept in her book and course of the same name. It's the 3 Rs[17]:

- **Reframe**: Feedback isn't facts about *you*; it's
  information about the giver's perspective.

17 Tara Mohr, "Navigating Feedback," https://www.taramohr.com/tools-and-inspiration-for-playing-bigger/navigating-feedback/

- **Relevance**: Decide whether it matters to your goals.

- **Revise**: Only then decide what (if anything) to change.

You have a choice. Take what serves you, and discard the rest thoughtfully and with care.

5. CHOOSE YOUR BEING AND DOING

Last, and not least, is the concept of Being and Doing.

I was introduced to this by the Co-Active Training Institute and it's changed my life and has improved the way I teach a lot of management topics.

Doing: These are the actions we're taking.

Being: This is our presence, how we show up.

Most of us are pretty good at thinking about the Doing. This is where we identify, *"I'm going to say this, do that, prioritize this, or address that."*

We can elevate our Doing by consciously considering our Being. How do I need to *be* when I do the *do*?

In the context of receiving feedback, we can lean into this concept. Ask yourself two questions:

1. What do I want to *do* when I receive feedback?

2. How do I want to *be* when I receive feedback?

Your response to the first question might be along the lines of, *"I want to ask follow-up questions and gain clarity, so I can understand how to take action."*

To the latter, you might consciously decide that you want to be calm, open, and nonjudgmental.

When you mindfully identify how you want to *be* and what you want to *do*, you'll find greater empowerment and intentionality within the situation.

CHAPTER SUMMARY

When we're given feedback, we have a responsibility to receive it with as much grace and curiosity as we can, even if it's delivered poorly. Is it 100% on our shoulders to receive well? No, we need those delivering feedback to also bear ownership for the role they play in the dynamic.

To better equip you for receiving feedback, below are five actions to practice:

1. **Understand your tendencies**: Be aware of your default reaction, and identify what helps you move toward change to ease the pressure of receiving feedback.

2. **Thank, Own, Ask**: Use this in real time to pause the interaction to regain your composure.

3. **Master your mindset**: Notice your assumptions and how your inner narrative is serving you (or not).

4. **Take some; leave some**: Know that every piece of feedback does not have to be implemented, so determine how feedback should be prioritized.

5. **Choose Being and Doing**: Proactively identify how you want to *be* and what you want to *do* when you receive feedback.

COMPLEMENTING YOUR EFFORTS WITH AI

In our increasingly hybrid, remote, virtual, and AI-influenced world, I would be remiss if I did not suggest guidance on how you might use AI to complement your feedback interactions.

The key word here is *complement*.

AI is enabling companies to streamline processes and increase efficiencies, opening up bandwidth for humans to do our uniquely human work.

Performance, career development, and employee engagement conversations—all instances where thoughtful and actionable feedback help you effectively manage your people—will continue to remain inherently human experiences.

The time, effort, and mental rigor you've put into learning the hows and the whys for having impactful conversations will serve you well. This cannot be replaced by AI.

That said, specific exchanges with AI can serve as a thought partner and sounding board to further refine your thinking and hone in on your messaging if and when you need it.

USING AI CHATBOTS

The quality of your inputs with Claude, Gemini, etc. will directly impact the outputs.

With too general of a prompt, you're at risk of gaining too many suggestions, leaving the situation more murky than it was before.

You can take clear and concise concepts from this book to inform the quality of your prompts, so the results strengthen your approach.

For example, you might use a chatbot to help you clarify your Name It to Tame It.

Imagine a prompt like this:

I am preparing to have a feedback conversation with a team member who I've identified has a career growth opportunity. To increase the clarity of my message and help with mutual understanding, I'd like your help brainstorming neutral terms that I could use that will encapsulate the performance or behaviors I'm seeking to help them improve.

Here is the situation . . .

[Describe the performance you're witnessing. It's okay to share your unfiltered perspective of the situation.]

Here's a bit about this person . . .

[Share insights into their style, preferences, and previous patterns of how they've received feedback in the past.]

Can you suggest 3–5 options for words or phrases (that are 1–3 words in length) that translate the narrative I've provided into a neutral representation of the skills or behaviors to be named in this feedback conversation?

From the suggested words and phrases you receive in response, you can apply your human discernment and knowledge of this person and their history to identify which Name It to Tame It to use in your conversation.

AI thought partnership, complemented by your own discernment, can support your confidence.

Here is another example.

Perhaps you're feeling stumped on your Headline. With clear guidance and a detailed prompt, you can use the tactics you've learned to seek brainstorming support. Here is a sample prompt:

I'd like your thought partnership to ensure my tone and word selection for an upcoming feedback conversation lands as intended.

My focus is crafting the headline (opening) for the conversation. A good headline focuses on their self-interest, sends a message of good intent, asks their permission for their time, and names the topic I want to discuss.

I've drafted the following headline . . .

[Paste what you've already crafted.]

The tone I want to strike is caring, invested, and direct. The part I'm unsure about is . . .

[Share your source of hesitation on your current word choices.]

Can you provide 3–4 suggestions to strengthen what I've already crafted?

The interactions you have with AI can also be opportunities for gathering feedback for yourself. When you seek brainstorming help, like the two examples above, it's an opportunity for you to reflect and learn from the advice offered.

AI NOTETAKING

In many organizations, particularly with remote-first employees, AI notetaking is quite common on video conferencing calls.

When you've shared feedback in a meeting that had automated notes, it can be useful for you to check whether you delivered actionable feedback. Do the notes reflect the actions the person will take as a result of your performance or development conversation?

This can be one way to use AI to hold yourself accountable to actionable feedback.

On the other hand, I would not depend on summary AI notes for your post-conversation feedback documentation needs. Part of the intention with a post-conversation email recap is having them respond. AI notetaking doesn't serve that function.

If you do choose to leverage AI notetaking for your virtual calls, please align with your people on the purpose.

I was testing using AI in my coaching sessions to more easily provide me a summary after each session. One person who was on the verge of sharing a big decision they'd made, paused and asked if it was okay to stop the notetaking. They shared, *"I'm wary of what AI might do with what I say, and I don't want to feel like I can't be honest."*

It's important to recognize that recording is a variable that can impact one's psychological safety.

NEXT STEPS IN AI

At the time of first publishing *Fearless Feedback*, many companies and HR teams were incorporating AI into their processes, including the following: AI suggestions for written performance reviews, spotting flight risks of high performers, or providing real-time coaching to managers on their tone in direct messages or email.

While much of AI is being built as we speak, we should take to heart this powerful quote from *Still Human: How to Build Organizations Where Leaders and Teams Thrive with AI*[18]:

> The human override principle is the idea that people always retain the authority to question, pause, or override automated or AI-driven decisions, especially when those decisions affect people's lives, opportunities, or well-being.

> Valuable feedback conversations that pull people in, help them grow, and enable them to deliver stronger results will always be human first and AI augmented.

CHAPTER SUMMARY

AI can complement your efforts, particularly in the realm of thought partnership and strengthening your drafts. You, as a human, are only going to become more important in an AI-driven world as your ability to engage, develop, and motivate performance will remain essential human experiences.

---

18 Bijal Choksi & Bonnie Davis, *Still Human: How To Build Organizations Where Leaders and Teams Thrive with AI*, 2026

CONCLUSION

You've done it! You've invested time and valuable energy to become a stronger, more impactful manager.

I set out to give you the tools you'd need to have meaningful feedback conversations and to highlight the nuances that separate good from great managers.

From three core frameworks (Fearless Feedback, HOA, and HEAR) to nuanced skills such as secondhand feedback, navigating reactions, documentation, and asking for feedback, we've covered a lot. Managers are not typically taught these skills.

In the Introduction, I asked you to rate yourself on two questions. It's time to loop back and notice what's changed. On a scale of one to five, what's your updated rating?

- Overall comfort giving specific critical feedback

- Level of stress and anxiety approaching a feedback conversation

What, specifically, have you noticed has shifted in your relationship with feedback? Honor and celebrate your own growth and development.

Now you have an opportunity to take things further.

1. Deepen development through conversation. Will you identify your top three takeaways from *Fearless Feedback* and share in your next one-to-one with your manager?

2. Host a management book club. Will you use the Manager Discussion Guide at the end of this book to facilitate meaningful discussion within your management team?

3. Teach others in order to solidify your understanding. Will you lead a lunch and learn with more junior managers and teach them the Fearless Feedback Framework?

4. Prepare and deliver feedback. What's a performance situation that you could improve? What's a career development opportunity you can address? Craft your message and deliver it in the next week.

5. Revisit early and often. Many of these chapters were written with the intention to be reviewed any time you need clarity or a boost of confidence. Revisit chapters or examples as often as you need.

If you have questions as you continue on in your feedback journey, my inbox is available to you: katie@enduranceboss.com.

If you found this book impactful to you and your career, I'd greatly value you leaving a review wherever you bought this book. Your review will help other managers discover this work.

MANAGER DISCUSSION GUIDE: FEARLESS FEEDBACK

A powerful way to deepen your learning is to discuss what you've read. Get together with your management team and use these questions for a deep discussion.

1. Mindset is a key component of effective feedback conversations. What have you noticed has changed about your mindset with feedback?

2. *Fearless Feedback* positions feedback as information that helps someone be their best. In what ways does this shift in perspective help you? What's powerful about that shift?

3. Think about a time you received feedback that was poorly delivered. Using what you've learned, what frameworks, tactics, or tools could that manager have used to help their message land differently?

4. Reactions to feedback are described as "speed bumps." How have you historically handled emotional reactions from your team members, and what will you do differently going forward?

5. Feedback without action is simply criticism. After reading this book, what has shifted in how you think about making your feedback actionable? What does a more effective feedback conversation look like for you now compared to before?

6. When the personal impacts the professional is a top area of stress and challenge for many managers. You read about a powerful consideration—those fighting silent battles versus those who are vocal—what are you seeing differently about managing performance, accountability, and feedback when people have a lot going on personally?

7. Think about a time feedback you gave didn't land or wasn't implemented. What will you do differently next time as a result of what you've learned in *Fearless Feedback*? Why?

8. The book addresses nuanced situations like remote employees, secondhand feedback, and considerations for letting someone go. Which of these scenarios felt most impactful for where you are in your management journey?

9. It's time for the rubber to meet the road. If you committed to one concrete change in how you deliver feedback starting this week, what would it be — and what support or accountability would help you follow through?

10. Peer mentorship is a powerful tool. From what you've read and your own lived experiences, what advice do you want to offer others about how to have effective feedback conversations?

ACKNOWLEDGMENTS

I have so many key people to recognize as being part of the journey in bringing *Fearless Feedback* to life.

Conni Medina and Claudine Mansour, thank you for leading this rookie through her first publishing event. Your edits and designs have set this book apart.

Ali Merchant and Diana Lowe, thank you for paving the way and sharing your self-publishing journey with me. Your willingness and generosity to share your lessons were incredibly helpful.

Rachael Peacock, who has been on the *Fearless Feedback* journey with me since 2022. It's your brilliance in design that first helped me better articulate my frameworks.

Patrick Foley, thank you for taking my random texts and gut-checking various elements of this book. Thank you also for being a fantastic actor, bringing these conversations to video format. Let your mama know your name is in print!

Kelly Flowers and Andi Pérez, I'm so appreciative of you being the first eyes to help ensure I hit the most relevant topics for managers.

Nick Fiedler, Jon Vick, Regina Lynch, and Tina Puls, each of you offered both validation and important improvements that helped elevate the entire book. I'm grateful for your time, attention, and interest in making this book impactful for managers around the world.

Pete Hancock, thank you for not sugar coating and high-lighting how to increase the impact of my message.

Dan Hammond, you preach what you practice, and it's a privilege to watch you in action. I'm grateful for you jumping at the opportunity to be an early reader.

Bonnie Davis and Leah Stallone, my two partners in crime for my women's leadership retreats, you two gave the honest feedback I needed on my book.

Christie Hoffman, you are a national treasure for the world of HR. Thank you for always keeping it super real and being a huge supporter of this project.

Jami Zakem, you taught me everything I know, and I'm eternally grateful for the universe bringing our careers together.

Rebecca Verhoeff and Emily Luchsinger, thank you for offering both your perspective and unconditional support.

Lindsey Valone and Diana Schaffner, it's you two who are the reason this book exists. Every October, you help me to see what I'm capable of and have unwavering faith in my ability to succeed. I'm grateful beyond words.

To my mom, thank you for being the first to read the entire manuscript, warts and all, and to never doubt anything I've set my mind to. My independence and success is a credit to you.

To all my sisters, thank you for celebrating each text update I sent. There is no me without you.

Last and not least, to my husband, Alex. The excited questions about how much I'd written and the unwavering support. You've helped me become an author. Time to pop a bottle of Taittinger!

ABOUT THE AUTHOR

Katie O'Brien Ceccarini is the founder of Endurance Management Coaching and has spent more than two decades leading, managing, and training people managers.

She started out in early education and then pivoted to tech where she helped scale and take two companies public. Now, trusted by Fortune 500 companies to train and coach their managers, Katie has built a reputation for being an expert in teaching others how to have difficult conversations.

When she's not developing our next generation of people managers, she's riding her horse, training as a triathlete, or hanging out with her son and husband in Denver.

To receive practical management and leadership actions every Friday, subscribe to her Substack, *The Lasting Leader*.